The Future of Customer Service

Published by Online Customer Care
P.O Box 122
Glen Gardner, NJ 08826

ISBN-13: 9781482065732
ISBN-10: 1482065738

First Edition: April 2013
Printed in the United States of America

Table of Contents

Introduction

You never change things by fighting the existing reality. To change something, build a new model that makes the existing model obsolete.

Buckminster Fuller

Thanks to Ptolemy the Greek, most of the civilized world once believed that the Earth was at the center of the universe. It was a mistake to question this wisdom – a person could easily be accused of heresy. When Galileo finally convinced enough influential people that we were just a very remote and tiny part of the cosmos, our entire concept was disrupted. So it is with modern customer service. One day we will look back at the way most businesses provided service during the early 21st century – annoying voice prompts, interminable queues and unempowered front line agents - and wonder how we could have accepted such a model.

The Future of Customer Service

Price and quality being regarded as equal, it is often the *perception* of the customer that determines whether or not any company is providing a product or service worthy of loyalty. In other words, a business must first understand the driving forces that make today's level of service such a key to commercial success.

Nothing is more frightening to an innovative company than the threat of a product or service becoming a *commodity*. Yet with globalization, this fear has become reality, and even the most powerful corporations in the world are being forced to adopt new ways of finding and retaining customers.

We still see marketing campaigns showing heroic customer service. The customer who forgets his brief case being pursued all the way to the aircraft by a smiling reservations agent; the financial services company who use a church bell to warn management that inbound call volume is too high and that it is time to log in and answer calls; the up-market clothing store that practices the belief that the customer is always right, even if that customer swears he bought a car battery in the Men's Department; the Baldrige Award winning company that uses over one hundred quality measurements at its call center; and so on. But is this truly the *essence* of customer service? What about this tribute once found in a major newspaper:

"We have looked for you as those who wait for the morning, and how seldom did you fail us! When days were months and hours weeks, how you thrilled us out of our pain and suspense, to know the best or know the worst! You have served us well!"

Most companies would flaunt that sort of testimonial from its customers. This one was written over 150 years ago as a tribute to a company we all know as the Pony Express. The company's service, which preceded the railway and only lasted a matter of a few weeks, was to deliver letters on horseback from one side of the United States to the other. The letters would often arrive late as well as damaged – perhaps because one of the agents had been ambushed or even killed along the way. The customer *perception* that this company was going above and beyond expectations that guaranteed its place as a service legend.

So what about a contemporary attempt to accomplish, if not the Pony Express standard, then at least service levels that maximize customer loyalty? It's not easy to inspire service legends when instead of heroes being attacked by bandits we have rows of closely monitored and often rigorously scripted agents sitting behind desks equipped with computers and telephones.

One problem is that in this era of global business and the Internet, 'the competition' is increasingly blurred and difficult to identify. Small to medium size companies are being forced to adopt not the Pony Express rider, but the marathon runner analogy, where they are competing not necessarily to beat anyone else, but to improve their own personal best: and in the process improve their position in the pack.

This book discusses the changes that visionary companies need to consider in order to remain on the cutting edge of service in a world where customers are becoming ever less trusting, and where the future of customer service will be driven by technological and social developments that will facilitate not only the fulfillment of a customer need for control and security, but also that will ultimately enable a restructuring of the entire model of employment and commerce as we know it today.

Introduction

In summary, this book first seeks to establish a benchmark for today's prevalent 'pseudo service', and then describes some of the criteria for what could be considered 'extreme service'. The importance of online communities and future emergence of 'tribal service' is then considered, as are the current trends and possible evolution of technology. Specifically, the role of reputation and reciprocity are examined, as well as the emergence of a barter economy. From a business perspective, particular attention is paid to myopic practices that place shareholders first and customers second, and what can be done to resolve this situation. The role of the contact center as the focal point of contemporary customer service is also given specific consideration.

The Future of Customer Service

Fundamentals

"This 'telephone' has too many shortcomings to be seriously considered as a means of communication. The device is inherently flawed."

Western Union Memo 1876

What's the real problem?

In 1935, when Robert W. Johnson, Jr., son of the man who founded Johnson & Johnson, first penned the company's credo, he committed the world's largest maker of healthcare products to an ideology of "enlightened self-interest," as he called it. That put service to customers first, service to employees and to management second and third, service to communities fourth, and service to stockholders, last. "When these things have been done," he wrote. "The stockholders should receive a fair return."

Today, with a few notable exceptions, major companies – those who historically have set the benchmark for excellence - pay only lip-service to the concept of delighting the customer. Business leaders are more concerned about managing shareholder expectations than meeting customer needs, often operating in a kind of parallel universe that has little to do with everyday reality, but everything to do with shareholder – not customer - perception.

After all, if a company is *perceived* to be maximizing shareholder value by whatever means necessary, then the stock price rises and executive management is rewarded accordingly. This is an approach that has indirectly led to the decline of true customer service and the rise of a 'pseudo service' driven only by diminishing operational budgets. After all, if the focus and energy of those at the top is largely on shareholder perception, then customers become a secondary concern. It is surmised that those companies who take the lead in reversing this trend will escape the collective wrath of 'tribal consumers' who are increasingly using the Internet and its social media arms to reveal and vilify those who have ignored the cornerstones of every successful business – the customers themselves.

It is not an exaggeration to say that today's typical big-business CEO is duty bound to meet shareholder expectations first, no matter what the cost to the customer and the common good. By doing what is necessary to positively shape investor sentiment, today's CEO stands to dwarf the salary - and even the bonus - that was originally attributed to his or her everyday job in the 'real' world. For the major corporate players who dominate global commerce, why focus purely on the realities of operational excellence, product innovation and customer intimacy when the rewards are so much greater and level of effort so much less 'granular' if shareholder expectations are carefully managed? Not only that, but the threat of capital losses from accounting rules attributed to a significant share price drop can force CEOs to work harder on bolstering shareholder perceptions than focusing on every day business.

Given this preoccupation with shareholder returns, the physical customer becomes an afterthought to many publicly traded companies. Instead, the person who should matter most has been left with a form of false service that belies what Peter Drucker once called the 'only one valid definition of a business purpose', that is, 'to create a customer'.

This problem is so rooted in contemporary commerce that to return to the ideal state where the customer is the focal point of business is almost akin to overturning the modern definition of capitalism. In a society where news on the trials and tribulations of the stock market is considered a benchmark for the wellbeing of an entire nation, it seems almost naïve to believe that 'proper' order as espoused by Robert W. Johnson, Jr. can be restored. To truly rectify the situation, companies must place customers, not shareholders, at the heart of their business strategy. Without such an approach, corrupt - or at least inappropriate - practices continue to flourish and business longevity becomes highly unlikely, at least not without the now ubiquitous merger or acquisition.

A myopic focus on meeting shareholder expectations could be seen as the antithesis of creating a meaningful bond with customers. It is a zero-sum world where imaginations, not realities, are expected to be fulfilled for the benefit of a select few. The price of failure for any business leader in such a world is certain oblivion, so why would any self-preserving CEO pay more attention to such outcomes than to pleasing the 'real' customer?

To take it a step further, what of the moral value of a company? What of the employees who are at the heart of the business? David Packard, founder of Hewlett-Packard once said, "Why are we here? I think many people assume wrongly, that a company exists simply to make money. Money is an important part of a company's existence, if the company is any good. But a result is not a cause. We have to go deeper, and find the real reason for our being. As we investigate this, we inevitably come to the conclusion that a group of people get together and exist as an institution that we call a company so that they are able to accomplish something collectively that they could not accomplish separately – they make a contribution to society, a phrase which sounds trite but is fundamental."

The economist Milton Friedman once said, "The question is, do corporate executives, provided they stay within the law, have responsibilities in their business activities other than to make as much money for their stockholders as possible? And my answer to that is, no, they do not...however, if socially responsible executives would stop and think, they would recognize that in effect they are acting irresponsibly."

Friedman believed in the application of capitalism to achieve as much profit as possible. In so doing, stockholders would be justly rewarded for their investments, and the community at large would benefit from a desirable product or service. Companies who advocated their sense of social responsibility, such as oil companies who ran advertising campaigns about saving the environment, were hypocrites, he espoused. An advocate of free economy, he also believed that companies engaged in damaging practices would be hurt by social and moral values, thus allowing the free market to "provide a much more sensitive and subtle voting mechanism than the political system".

Today, the problem with Friedman's view is that we no longer deal with a responsibly controlled supply and demand marketplace. Globalization has unleashed a new and willing labor market in places most of us have never heard of, let alone thought of as an engine of global commerce. This cheap, willing, or coerced workforce is unlikely to care whether they are making napalm or paper handkerchiefs. Moral and social values are not generally part of the mass production agenda. The object, which Friedman would certainly condone, is to make as much money, and gain as much technical knowledge, in the shortest time possible.

What Friedman might not condone, however, is that these tasks should be accomplished with little or no regard for consequence.

Before delving into the social and technological future of customer service, it's worth looking at what can be done from the outset to shift the focus from short-term shareholder demands to the needs of the actual customer. According to Roger L. Martin, there are several courses of action that can be taken. One is the repeal of 1995 Private Securities Litigation Reform Act, which contains the infamous "safe harbor" provision. Without this provision, executives and their companies could be legally liable for any attempt to manage expectations – specifically, the practice of 'earnings guidance'. Another is the elimination of regulation FASB 142 which forces the real write-downs of real assets based on the company's share price in the expectations market. The current rule forces executives to concern themselves with managing expectations in order to avoid write-downs. Changing the rule would remove the major sanction that now exists for executives who ignore the expectations market. A third suggestion is the elimination of stock-based compensation as an incentive to CEOs. Martin also suggests the regulation of hedge funds, while others point to reinstating the value of the worker through the elimination of practices such as sweatshop outsourcing, reduced benefits, pension fund depletion, and even re-establishing the concept of 'delighting the customer', which in turn will realize not only huge returns on investment for the company, but also for the common good.

The Importance of Trust

Once the focus of a company is where it should be, a key to any reciprocal arrangement between the enterprise and its customers is the existence of *trust*. Without trust, business transactions become stuck in small details and endless complaints. After all, it is from trust that we find the key to customer loyalty. The problem is that in this age where the customer is rarely seen – what we might call the *Age of the Invisible Customer* – establishing trust is often a very tough task.

From the perspective of customer retention, practices in the vast majority of contemporary customer service offerings are analogous to the Emperor's new clothes – everybody knows that they make no sense, but few are willing to admit that change is essential. In truth, contemporary "toll free" customer service is an oxymoron.

Companies are mimicking one another in an effort to keep pace, but nobody is stating the fact that true service has very little to do with commerce. From a consumer perspective, it could be argued that unless it somewhat fulfills a basic human need, the product or service is relatively meaningless *unless* it allows differentiation or even a form of 'self-actualization' to take place at the individual level.

Money is a fundamental example of the importance of trust. "The root problem with conventional currency," says Satoshi Nakamoto, the alleged creator of Bitcoin, the virtual currency of the Internet, "is all the trust that's required to make it work. The central bank must be trusted not to debase the currency, but the history of fiat currencies is full of breaches of that trust. Banks must be trusted to hold our money and transfer it electronically, but they lend it out in waves of credit bubbles with barely a fraction in reserve. We have to trust them with our privacy, trust them not to let identity thieves drain our accounts."

A similar model of trust is required for all of commerce. The customer must always trust that the company has not compromised the original quality of the product or changed the parameters of service since we purchased the original that made us come back for more. The customer must also trust that if anything goes wrong, the company will make it right, preferably without making us stay on hold for an hour, or answer interminable questions, or print and fill out forms, or provide personal information in order to obtain a refund, or be 'offered' a new and improved version for a little more commitment of time, money and business intelligence. Yet how valid is such an approach with a corporate establishment who are barely able to contain their enthusiasm for monopolies and powerful lobbying?

Even when a certain measure of trust has been established, customers expect a problem to be resolved quickly. The modern practice of attempting to cut costs by offering post sale telephone, email and chat services that are designed to placate customers rather than resolve real issues on the first point of contact is both arcane and apt to do more harm than good. Putting friendly humans on the front lines with carefully scripted responses but little or no authority is an industrial age approach doomed to obsolescence. Instead, companies must empower agents to act quickly and decisively.

Typically, those who are most concerned about 'giving away the shop' by empowering the front lines are the least likely to condescend to resolving real time customer problems. The traditional attitude might be: 'that kind of stuff is handled by our call center on the other side of the world, which by the way costs us $x per year to maintain, or x% of our operational budget. If I can lower that percentage next year, I'll be looking at a nice bonus.' In the same discussion, one is likely to hear something akin to 'We are also looking for ways to further cut costs by speeding up talk times and re-directing as many contacts as possible to the automated system.'

The future of customer service dictates that the attitude of successful companies is more likely to be: 'If the front line agent can't reach a supervisor to resolve a complex customer problem, then he or she needs to be empowered to make the decision themselves. After all, if management want to influence the decision of a subordinate, then they are expected to keep their lines of communication open at all times – no excuses.'

The rise of grid computing and mobile technologies already allow more customers to share more positive or negative information about a company more quickly than anyone living twenty years ago could have envisioned. Just as responsive companies will be praised as standard-bearers for the new economy, antiquated approaches to customer service will be seized upon and vilified by 'virtual tribes' of customers whose influence carries to interested parties across the entire planet in a matter of seconds.

The faceless nature of corporations means that by design, there will always be an 'us and them' mentality. Corporations are designed to maximize profit while at the same time creating an aura of cooperation for the common good. Even those that manage to appease anonymous shareholder demands for maximum return on investment while at the same time enhancing their reputation for customer service, are under increased pressure to balance these competing approaches as we enter this new era of customer assertiveness.

The following chapters explore the challenges facing companies that wish to place the customer front and center, the obvious benefits of doing so, and as some would argue, the inevitable consequences for those who do not.

The Future of Customer Service

Pseudo Service

From a very early age, we're taught to break apart problems - to fragment the world. This apparently makes complex tasks and subjects more manageable. But we pay a hidden, enormous price – we can no longer see the consequences of our actions. We lose our intrinsic sense of connection to a larger whole. When we then try to see the "big picture", we try to reassemble the fragments in our minds, to list and organize all the pieces. But the task is futile. It's similar to trying to reassemble the fragments of a broken mirror to see a true reflection. So after a while we give up trying to see the whole altogether.

Peter Senge

A smile on the face of a limousine driver is no substitute for the automobile.

Michael Hammer

Today, in an age of mass consumption and commodity products, service is generally defined as something that functions as a competitive differentiator. In other words, it is something that allows a company, group or individuals to become more valued by an element of human society, and therefore worthy of some form of trust or even loyalty. Usually, this definition is applied to the usage of a product or service which fulfills a perceived need. First tier business endeavors, for instance, will include the harnessing of natural resources for the manufacture of steel, heavy machinery, wood products, and other materials. This creates the framework for contemporary living through the construction and manufacturing industries. On the consumer products side, these fundamentals evolve into electrical appliances, automobiles, clothing, food, luxury goods, and so on. In turn, these products demand services such as electricity, banking, transportation, insurance, entertainment, and a host of others.

Yet despite these outputs of the industrial age, are we to surmise that "service" is purely a by-product of increased human capability? It is interesting to compare contemporary service demands to Maslow's "Hierarchy of Needs", in which humans move from physiological needs, to desires for safety, social acceptance, self-esteem, and ultimately, self-actualization. Once the fundamental needs for clothing, food and shelter have been fulfilled, Maslow asserted that we begin to explore new avenues of fulfillment – states of being that can only be accomplished through greater affluence. The poor man will take whatever food and shelter he can acquire, without any particular expectation of quality, whereas the rich man will strive to be recognized as such, perhaps through the acquisition of material goods. Despite a plethora of modifications and the emergence of compelling terms like "loyalty", "partnership" and "intimacy", the business world by its nature resolutely adheres to the myopic notion that people are purely interested in self-gratification even if the future of their children and humankind in general, may be in question.

The focus on the overall "customer experience" did not emerge until very recently. Today's "buzz" words are important to business because the products and services that once astounded the world can rapidly become commodities in an ever more competitive commercial arena. Yet the customer service experience has undoubtedly been around since the first signs of man's desire to fulfill these needs. In the era when cowry shells were used as capital, the individual who collected the most beautiful shells probably competed with the one who could deliver poorer quality shells in less time, or was awed by the first one who recognized the niche market for ornate necklaces to display the cowries.

The Future of Customer Service

If it is accepted that service is simply something that encourages a stronger sense of customer satisfaction, then we will continue to use it as part of a marketing strategy which embraces tried and trusted ways of contained low cost care, such as the provisioning of toll-free telephone numbers for pre and post-sale support, streamlined fulfillment processes, warranty assurances and 'no questions asked' returns. Inherently, such a strategy has nothing to do with matters beyond the relative satisfaction conveyed to the customer via the product or service.

Taking this a step further delves into the much vaunted realm of customer loyalty. Not only has the customer purchased a good product, but he or she is subliminally encouraged by the brand name advertisements that appear in several media, espousing the class and social standing of this product's customer base. A free call to the company is answered by a pleasant and cooperative representative. A glossy color catalog arrives in the mail. Personalized online account service makes a customer's decision to swap for a different style a simple exercise. Overall, the company effuses cooperation and partnership. They are intimately aware of the customer's needs. Now that's service! Or is it?

The reality is that affluent consumers of industrialized nations who continue to make up the majority of target markets will have to be retained in the future through *extraordinary* loyalty initiatives. This will mean real "partnering" with the customer - not just to meet self-serving needs, but to present products and services which *holistically* compete in a global sense. Such differentiation will be based not just on price and product quality, but on the premise of what could be termed, in a Maslovian sense, self-actualization.

To achieve differentiation, multinational companies may even have to nurture a mindset whereby consumers perceive themselves to be truly concerned and involved in the entire production and distribution process, as well as the esteem associated with the acquisition of the product or service. In order to achieve this, altruistic marketing strategies will be reinforced, ironically, via the same public relations, advertising, lobbying, and news media channels that once held firm to concept of the self-indulgent consumer. Instead these powerful manipulators will develop a strong public consciousness of the "deteriorating global infrastructure". The outcome will be that long-established companies will have to be seen as throwing open their proprietary doors to embrace the common good.

Pseudo CRM

Today, even when useful information is provided by the customer, very little is recorded, and far less is used. Segmentation based on revenue generation alone builds picket fences around criminals and philanthropists alike. The despot who spends a lot of money on the company's product or service will naturally continue to command far greater appeal than the low-spending philanthropist who just donated millions of dollars to preserve the rain forest. After all, that is the nature of capitalism. Yet is this what customer relationship management is all about? The conclusion might be that the company organized solely around income as a differentiator is innately flawed – but should a corporation make moral judgments? The obvious answer is no. The question is will this ever change?

Most companies today use call centers as a means to provide customer service. These operations are typically referred to as cost centers. Historically, the less the company has to spend on the call center, the more profit is generated.

Hence many centers today are found offshore, in countries that offer cheap multi-lingual labor and low overhead costs. However, as they embrace responsibility for faster, more pervasive and powerful customer channels such as social media, it is becoming clear that companies who fail to see the evolution of these important touch points into a 'contact center' for the overall customer experience, do so at significant risk.

The modern 'contact center' is a microcosm of business, and far more complex and challenging than an outsider might imagine. Important service facilitators such as IVR scripting, CTI implementation, skills-based routing, queue management, call tracking, workflow support, knowledge engineering, workforce management and reporting, as well as recruiting, training, incenting and retaining employees, make up the fundamental attributes of the contact center. Adding the complexities of the new economy – end-to-end support, VoIP, e-mail, universal business applications, collaboration, chat, call through, call back, and so on ...we find that these centers are no longer fulfilling just a pre and post-sale support function, but becoming the critical link in the entire supply chain, performing a centralized sales function, fulfilling orders, supporting self-service functions, answering inquiries, distributing marketing information, and solving problems and complaints.

In the midst of such complexity, it is sometimes easy to become entirely focused on metrics that can easily be attributed to bottom line costs – average speed of answer, talk time, and abandonment rate. These are, after all, the kind of measurements that we can use to show management just how much it costs to support customers on a day-to-day basis. Yet critical though these aspects may be, they are not what really interest the majority of those involved in customer-facing operations.

Yet in the words of authors Don Peppers and Martha Rogers: "Linear, operational data drives most traditional call centers, in large measure because they're viewed as cost centers (reduce talk time 7%, improve customer satisfaction 8%, decrease call-abandonment rate to 9%). The CFOs and COOs who oversee the call center only glance occasionally at any data not related to cost-per-station or cost-per-call. Quite often they have no real clue about the potential marketing and relationship-building power hiding in that small, expensive, often problematic business unit in the basement."

Even companies who operate the best call centers cannot always delight the customer. Such an objective is a very expensive one, and therefore companies must be selective as to whom they attempt to delight. As one VP of Customer Service put it: "I don't need to be *this* much (expands hands) better than the competition, I just need to be *this* much (thumb and forefinger)!"

The Evolution of Service

The evolution of service can perhaps be explained using game theory. This suggests that people will act in a rational manner by choosing an approach to existence that will maximize their gain regardless of the consequences to others. For example, should a company bother to provide exceptional service to another business that is going bankrupt? What is the reward for doing so? In contrast, should a company go out of its way to reward those customers who have demonstrated loyalty and a willingness to part with a relatively meaningful amount of capital, in anticipation of maintaining a profitable ongoing relationship?

Game theory assumes that conflict exists, that participants will take action, and the results of those actions will determine which participant benefits according to definite rules. At the core of this notion is the theory of *cooperation*. In other words, humans (and corporations) will cooperate more fully with each other when there is the prospect of a gainful relationship. What stops the participants from acting entirely selfishly is the establishment of *reputation*. Reputation stems from repetition – if the person or corporation believes it is likely that a business transaction will be repeated in some form or other in the future, then there is less likelihood of trickery or dismissive behavior when a claim for retribution is made (e.g., when a customer claims that a product was broken when it arrived, or that a charge was made erroneously on their account). Hence the importance of understanding a customer's history, such as it exists, when contact is made.

Along the same lines, the owner of the village store can evaluate us at a glance. Psychologist Albert Merabian writes that in the "realm of feeling" our "facial and vocal expressions, postures, movements and gestures" are crucial. When our words "contradict the messages contained within them, others mistrust what we say – they rely almost completely on what we do." …eye contact, gestures (both intentional and unintentional), nods, a faint furrowing of the brow, body language, seating arrangements, even hesitation measured in milliseconds - none of this mass of information that we ordinarily process almost without thinking in face-to-face encounters is captured in a typical call center transaction.

The village store owner can become very familiar with our buying habits, how often we return to the store, what kind of purchasing ability we possess, how open we are to cross-selling and other profit-making suggestions, what our personal and economic situation at any given time might be, and so on. Our lifetime value is very evident, as is our influence over others, our complaint power and even our nuisance factor. As an easily recognized member of the community, the village store owner gains our trust through repeated transactions and personal respect.

The average call center agent, on the other hand, certainly doesn't know that Jim is anxious because he is going through a divorce, or that Laura is exhausted because her father is dying, or that John is lonely because he is living three thousand miles from home. The customer relationship management system, no matter how sophisticated, is not built to empathize with the human condition. Significance, self-worth, security, convenience and especially empathy, are the characteristics that service companies must convey to their customers in order to achieve the elusive goal of loyalty. Yet behavioral science has been strangely absent from the realm of call centers.

Contemporary customer service is often conducted between individuals who sit halfway around the globe. Both parties are aware that they will probably never speak to each other again. The call center agent is constrained by policies and procedures that must be followed in order to remain gainfully employed. The caller, on the other hand, may or may not be concerned about the agent's perception of their behavior – a consideration that could involve (a) obtaining a desired outcome and/or (b) concern about the ramifications of overt behavior. Today, when we contact customer service via telephone, the interaction is immediately unnatural in that we are speaking to a microphone and listening to a speaker that has no physical presence.

Customers are known to be less inhibited in the faceless world of modern customer service. This is known as the 'disinhibition' effect. Terms such as 'disassociative anonymity' are used by psychologists to explain why many customers feel they can behave much differently on the telephone than in face-to-face conversations. It is a conviction that whatever they say to 'John' or 'Jane' at the call center can't be directly linked to their 'real' life. When acting out hostile feelings, the customer doesn't have to take responsibility for those actions. The invisibility of the transaction adds to the perceived anonymity and encourages the caller to be far more expressive and demanding than he or she would be in face-to-face transactions. It could be concluded that the anonymity of remote interactions that do not involve visual personification allow individuals to perceive these as a kind of game with rules and norms that don't apply to everyday living.

As technology facilitates virtual face-to-face transactions between customers and agents, regardless of geographical location, a number of critical questions arise, including whether visual transactions will lower talk times and also decrease unreasonable customer demands for financial compensation by encouraging 'normal' social behavior. This has huge implications from a cost perspective, particularly when considering high volume contact centers. By incenting customers with high speed Internet capabilities to use the face-to-face medium, perhaps simply through sidestepping

IVR functions and ACD queues, companies may find that cost per contact drops significantly.

A neglected area in service provisioning has been the building of agent competence in the area of focused, evaluative listening. For example, although deprived of visual cues, the perceptive and competent agent is able to "see" customer expressions, hear the subtle clues and accurately gauge an appropriate response to the customer.

Realistically, however, in an era of high agent turnover and in the context of the invisible customer, we must rely largely on computer systems to rapidly retrieve expert information and present it to the agent in a way that is instantly understandable. Just as the village store owner knows the cost, quantity and location of virtually every item in stock, so too must the system facilitate the agent by providing an integrated view of the entire business. And just as the store owner knows his or her regular customers by name and background, so too must the system be populated with information that can tell the agent at a glance exactly who the customer is and why they have contacted the company in the past.

Similarly, the agent must be able to recognize and act upon opportunities to embrace new business by presenting options to the customer in a timely manner. Recognizing that agents, unlike the village store owner, are not typically decision-makers, the system must also enable company management to extract meaningful business intelligence, which in turn may be profitably used to drive strategic management initiatives.

A key question today, therefore, is how to empower agents by providing them with the sort of information and authority which will make every worthy customer feel as though the company cares about them personally, thus establishing the bond of trust. This goal is clearly a complex task that involves a multitude of processes and, depending on the size of the customer base, significant technological support. It may never equate to the village store, but done properly it is enough to provide that small, but crucial competitive edge mentioned earlier.

And here is where many companies are making their biggest mistake. A popular business concept like CRM, for example, is too often translated to mean Cost Reduction Management, and may have about as much to do with establishing and maintaining customer trust as reducing talk time in a call center has to do with quality.

Cost cutting strategies, often to meet shareholder demands for short-term profit, are a reality in today's business environment. The good news for call centers is that new economy will continue to transform their business role and the relative importance of those who work there, by pushing multi-channel customer communications into a centralized, highly visible profit-making entity that we now call the "Contact Center".

Even in traditional call center operations, customer service professionals often have to achieve the difficult balance of not only gaining customer trust, as we have discussed, but also demonstrating a very real contribution to corporate profitability. While gaining customer trust is often a long-term endeavor, the modern approach to profitability is often measured by quarter-to-quarter earnings. So how do we achieve both of these often conflicting goals?

The obvious answer for any centralized customer contact operation is investment in technology, but before doing so, there are some basic questions to be answered.

Firstly, management has to decide whether the company is in the business of creating actual long-term *relationships* with customers or whether it just needs to provide efficient, inexpensive, convenient, friendly customer service on an as needed basis.

While one-to-one relationship building is often touted as a customer service solution for all companies, no matter what the product or service offering, this is simply not true. An important distinction must be made between efficiency-based and relationship-based customer service. There are certain situations in which we expect and want nothing more than efficiency and convenience. Buying a meal at a fast-food restaurant; shopping for light bulbs; buying petrol; purchasing a toaster; and so on. These are all efficiency-based services that do not typically require the establishment of an ongoing relationship with the customer.

By following the one-to-one relationship philosophy, many efficiency-based companies have been trying to develop what have been termed "pseudo-relationships" with customers. When I call in for the third time looking for a replacement control pad for my son's video game and have been sitting in queue for twenty minutes, do I really want the agent to greet me by my first name, review my purchasing history, and try to cross-sell other products? Not a chance! The fact is that unless the information being gathered and used is directly beneficial to me as a customer, this type of pseudo-relationship approach can actually damage my view of the company.

However, there are other relationship-based situations in which as a customer we may come to expect special treatment. On a recent trip to Europe to research outsourced call centers, for example, a client decided to fly business class. As one might expect, the fare was very expensive, but in return the airline added *unexpected* value by providing a concierge who came to meet the client as soon as he identified himself, took his baggage and paperwork, helped him through customs, escorted him to the executive lounge, came back to get him when it was time to board, and even helped him to locate his seat on the aircraft. A few days later, the concierge sent a follow up thank you card. In return, the client sent a letter to the company CEO praising both the employee and the airline. Now that budgets have been cut and he is back to flying economy class, that airline is still his first choice, because it took the trouble to establish a good old-fashioned relationship with him.

Yet even in a relationship-based situation, how do companies figure out which customers are worthy of special attention? After all, customer segmentation is a risky business. Loyal and profitable customers are relatively easy to identify with appropriately configured CRM systems, but a far greater challenge is to build a reliable profile of the profit-making potential of every customer, especially when consumer concerns regarding privacy are reaching an all-time high. The standard response by companies to objections from customers for more personal information is, "The more you tell us, the better we'll be able to serve you." This is true, but not sufficient. An individual can't comfortably provide information unless there is trust – the first part of the equation we discussed.

For trust to exist, customers need to know who knows about them, and the full details of what they know. After all, we don't want to follow the example of one major bank that drew a red line below those customers who had achieved a minimum bank balance for a certain period of time, and set up a CTI-enabled call center system to show different levels of value for each inbound caller – green for the most profitable customers and red for the others. Those who didn't get a green light were always dropped to the bottom of the queue and actively encouraged to use a rather poorly designed IVR. The problem was that some of the redlined customers were the sons and daughters of major investors, or university MBA students with enormous earning potential. When the story reached the front pages of the New York Times, the bank's image was seriously damaged.

If a company wants to provide personalized service to just a handful of customers, it can probably staff up with top agents to meet the demand, but if the target audience is far greater, then this is where one can really see systematic solutions emerge as a powerful force. After all, we are moving away from the notion of technology managing information and toward the idea of technology as a medium of relationships. In the words author Kevin Kelly: *"Despite the billions of bits of information that can be processed in a second, the only matter of consequence silicon produces are relationships."*

One of the key elements for any company thinking of investing in a CRM system is calculation of return on investment. Too many expensive CRM systems have been purchased without giving attention to this measurement. After all, without understanding the quantifiable improvement brought about by a CRM system, it is impossible to justify the investment, much less contribute to the company's profitability.

For example, call center time and motion studies both before and after systems implementation are a critical piece of measuring return on investment. Time *every* manual process that is likely to be impacted by the system. Quantifiable measurements of improvement in, for example, new agent training time frames, number of customer contacts required to resolve a situation, customer satisfaction and retention, and so on, will realize tangible measurements that can be translated into actual return on investment calculations.

For companies who still see the call center as a stand-alone operation, that's all the justification that is required to move forward. For those that are interested in customer relationship management, however, it's time to make sure that everyone else understands the value that such a solution can bring.

The first question is whether everyone in the company agrees about who the customer actually is? Secondly, are all company departments committed to implementing a system that requires cross-organizational input in order to ensure the return on investment? It is not unusual for multi-million dollar CRM systems being used appropriately by the call centre, but being viewed as nothing more than elaborate commitment tracking systems by field sales. Thirdly, does senior management understand and actively support the business processes that enable the distribution and analysis of customer information? The best CRM systems are designed to enable a company's front office support – sales, marketing and service - work together seamlessly to create a complete view of the customer. Yet not all decision-makers understand this premise. For example, one manufacturer wanted help in selecting a CRM system for their customer service facility. The consultant noticed that sales and marketing were conspicuously absent from the business case development meetings. When this was pointed out, the individual was told not to worry because those departments had just invested in another leading CRM package that was "much better at sales force automation than customer service."

Despite spectacular advances in technology, especially in the realm of centralized customer interaction, the information generated concerning the customer is only as good as that which is put into the system by everyone who comes into contact with that customer. For example, the gap between the information actually received from a customer, versus the information entered into the system, versus the information analyzed, versus the information actually used to improve the company's relationship with that customer, reveals that even the best systems rely on competent, motivated humans who are empowered by a strategic approach to customer service that permeates the entire company.

The Shorter-term Evolution of Service

As a radical example of the service concept run amok, in Aldous Huxley's *Brave New World* the author describes a Utopian society in which everything is provided for the benefit of the consumer who follows the rules implicitly. In return, the customer gives up any vestige of deeper values and pledges total allegiance to a faceless system of government. Is that what is meant by extreme service? Is that the end game of the current society?

Huxley writes about an entire society based around the "conscription of consumption", with the philosophy that "ending is better than mending". In stark contrast, Huxley's *savage*, who is a reviled outcast of such a society, raves about the existence of "the soul", much to the amusement of a 'controller', who is content to use the savage as an example of what happens to those who do not conform.

From a pure profit-making perspective, it could be surmised that the successful service strategy of tomorrow will deviate considerably from the capitalistic model that exists in today's industrialized nations. Unless protectionism and its advocates manage to arrest globalization, multinationals will be subject to increased competition from low cost, high output, and at least comparable quality manufacturers in emerging nations from the proverbial four corners of the earth. In order to avoid deflation via over-production of commodity goods and services, even the largest institutions and most popular brand names may have to adopt a dramatic and erstwhile unthinkable survival strategy that may even be known as *conscientious capitalism*.

Contemporary service 'for the common good' will continue to expand its horizons – a chemical company may boast about their latest environment-friendly detergent; a shoe manufacturer may boast about their high safety concerns in Malaysian factories; a cell phone company may tout their efforts to raise the minimum wage in the Philippines; telecommunications companies may partner to abolish unsightly over ground cable and minimize electro-magnetic exposure; a pharmaceutical company may enforce internal air pollution controls that far surpass the most stringent government regulations on the planet; a computer manufacturer may introduce computer component recycling plants, and so on. The majority of the cost, of course, will be passed on to the consumer, but only based on what the market will bear based on an "annihilation index". These companies will have to take a significant and unprecedented hit in order to create a "kinder, gentler world". Many will be unable to come to terms with this and will continue to compete on brand name alone – a short-term policy that will eventually be extinguished by the emergence of comparable service strategies within low cost competitors.

Low cost, high quality manufacturers from emerging nations will undoubtedly use existing channels in today's industrialized nations in order to provide some sort of service realization process, particularly for upper tier customers. This will involve significant trial and error, as cultural, social and language problems will result in a potential consumer backlash. The companies who grasp the evolving western paradigm of service will be the giants of tomorrow's global marketplace.

Service "industries", such as banking, insurance, utilities, finance, and telecommunications, will not go unscathed by the new model. Insurers, for example, will be pressured not to underwrite any policies that overtly could compromise global welfare, such as nuclear waste dumping, the use of cyanide in strip mining, toxic chemical plants in suburban areas, etc. Bankers will be pressured not to supply loans to similar industrialists. Utility companies will have to find widespread alternatives to fossil fuel burning, and so on.

From a consumer standpoint, the groundswell of concern about impending global calamities (i.e., greenhouse gases, ozone depletion, carcinogenic or unbreathable air, human rights deprivation, nuclear waste, etc.) will undoubtedly continue to grow, however, although it may take a real catastrophe to drive the point home. For business, on the other hand, the alternatives are rampant deflation or protectionism. The difference will be that the consumer society of industrialized nations will perceive the higher cost of "self-actualization" as a means for providing a better quality of life both for itself and future generations. Companies, meanwhile, will have to come to terms with a new business model which forces them to expose former wrongdoings and plausibly "immoral" practices which have now been embraced by emerging nations. The industrial giants of the 19th and 20th centuries will literally have to eat humble pie in order to "partner" with the consumer. The interesting thing about all this is that two historically opposing factions - environmentalists / human rights activists and multinational corporations, may become unlikely partners in the quest for an enhanced global quality of life.

Just as the economist John Maynard Keynes once wrote about "absolute" vs. "insatiable" needs, so too will the consumer of the future question the capitalistic dogma of "more is always better" by demanding products and services that minimally impact the environment, from companies who vigorously support the furtherance and improvement of human existence. Discretionary income will increasingly combine with corporate profit in order to establish a new sense of esteem – that which espouses a combination of philanthropy and newfound capitalistic consciousness.

The Future of Customer Service

We are already seeing an extraordinary transformation of the traditional call center. Technology is facilitating this change – but again it is critical to remember that it is the 'invisible' customer's level of trust, not the technology and not the medium, that is going to determine success or failure in the long run. As the sociologist Francis Fukuyama says: "trust does not reside in integrated circuits or fiber optic cables". *Trust is earned.* Future success will depend on enlightened, service-oriented leaders who allow their front line employees to practice the fine art of reciprocity. In this way, the best companies will be able to use customer service as a true business differentiator.

Extreme Service

"Here he comes! Away across the endless dead level of the prairie a black speck appears against the sky…sweeping toward us nearer and nearer…a whoop and a hurrah…a wave of the rider's hand…and man and horse burst past our excited faces, and go winging away like a belated fragment of a storm!"

Mark Twain

To elaborate a little more on the example of extreme service mentioned in the introduction, Mark Twain captured the excitement of the most dangerous customer service job in the west – the Pony Express rider. This was no chair-bound, script-laden, schedule-driven, headset touting call center position. In 1860, this much quoted Pony Express advertisement for representatives might have enjoyed a better response than it would get today:

"WANTED – Young, Skinny, Wiry fellows not over eighteen. Must be expert riders, willing to risk death daily. Orphans preferred".

Yet there were some parallels. For example, successful Pony Express candidates had to swear that "I will, under no circumstances, use profane language; that I will drink no intoxicating liquors; that I will not quarrel or fight with any other employee of the firm…So help me God." Today, those words might be translated to call center measurements of "courtesy, empathy, and reliability".

The most famous Pony Express riders were James Butler Hickok ("Wild Bill") and William Cody ("Buffalo Bill"). The latter of these two legends wrote of an event that even at fifteen years of age would surely have qualified him for "Agent of the Month" consideration:

One day when I galloped into Three Crossings, my home station, I found that the rider who was expected to take the trip out … had been killed; and that there was no one to fill his place. I did not hesitate for a moment to undertake an extra ride of eighty-five miles to Rocky Ridge, and I arrived…on time. I then turned back and rode to Red Buttes, my starting place…a distance of 322 miles.

In this era of grievances and wrongful dismissal claims, it is also interesting to note the type of treatment meted out to customer service agents who might have seen fit to take a little more from the company than was originally agreed upon. One such individual, Jules Reni, was suspected of such activities. The Pony Express division chief, Joseph Slade, responded by "filling him with lead by practiced degrees, starting with the extremities and working towards the vitals. When Jules finally sagged dead, Slade cut off his ears, nailing one to the corral post as a warning, and tanning the other for use as a watch fob".

It wasn't long before the astounding feats of Pony Express riders were dwarfed by technology in the form of the first transcontinental telegraph. This incredible innovation, completed on October 24th, 1861, sent its first message eastward to President Lincoln, assuring him of California's loyalty to the Union. In a few seconds, the communications device had transcended what had taken the ponies and their riders several days to accomplish. Within a few weeks, the owners of the Pony Express saw the writing on the wall, so to speak, and went out of business.

The company never made a profit and lasted only a short time before it was obliterated by technology, yet its legacy persists. Can we now look to modern technology – that which changed our expectations forever – to push us into a new era of customer service?

The Basics of Extreme Service

This is a book about the future of customer service. While we are still years away from some of the concepts discussed in this book, that doesn't mean we should only consider abstractions. Creating the future of customer service is a matter of changing the currently accepted norm, which in some people's minds generally sets the bar quite low. So what is "Extreme" service in the conservative sense? Here are some discussion points:

- Anticipating my requirements
- Empowering the front lines
- Recognizing my value as a customer
- Bartering my abilities for reciprocal goods and services

- Proactively following up on any outstanding issues on my behalf
- Taking my suggestions seriously
- Never making an unsolicited communication of any sort.
- Finding others with similar interests and experiences
- Advising me of issues that may impact my security.

Some of these service 'extremes' go well beyond what is offered today. Others seem more feasible, but are often given only lip service by companies today. As such, it is worth looking at each of these 'requirements' individually:

- **Anticipating my requirements**

  Whatever the channel or external touch point, if a customer has contacted the company previously, then whomever is dealing with the latest communication should have some systematic intelligence about the nature of that contact, whether the customer was unhappy with the product or service, whether it was resolved, whether it is likely to re-occur, whether the customer's request was reasonable, whether the client is open to suggestions on product or service enhancements, and so on. For example, if the customer has a history of re-ordering a certain number of a particular item, then this should be immediately apparent to the recipient, just as should any disclosure the customer has made that might influence the company's ability to maintain existing service levels. Without prompting, the agent should be able to state "I see that you increased your usage of international minutes / purchased our ultimate carbon fiber bicycle / had your head gasket replaced / completed our beginner course last month. Perhaps I can save you some time and money…"

Research has found that good customer service does not normally promote loyalty, but service that is perceived as 'bad' will cause significant churn. Resolving the customer's initial problem on the first contact is a good start, but anticipating and resolving future contacts *before these occur* is far better. For example, helping a customer register a product may be chalked up as 'resolved on first contact', but anticipating and addressing issues that may occur post-registration – such as a known common issue with a product or service - *on the same initial contact* is the essence of this aspect of extreme service.

- **Empowering the front lines**
  Don't put the customer through to a machine that is

designed to defray company costs by forcing that individual to answer a series of inane prompts and questions that provide only high level information and make it almost impossible to ever reach a human. Then when the customer reaches a human, don't ask that person to repeat the information the machine already requested and don't give the customer to someone who is merely following a specific script and has no authority to actually resolve anything. If the machine actually has a function that provides value in a matter of seconds, then no problem. If the human picks up the communication within a minute or so, has a strange accent and lives halfway across the planet, but is actually empowered to resolve legitimate customer problems, then that is also acceptable. If the company is measuring the effectiveness of the front lines solely by minimizing the number of minutes spent engaging the customer, then it has no business referring to the transaction as 'customer service'.

Training the front lines never to answer in negatives such as 'we don't' or 'we can't' to 'we will' has been found to reduce customer defections, as well as training agents to understand the type of customer they are dealing with is also perceived as a form of empowerment. For example, based on verbal cues from the outset of the call, apart from the obvious irate or frustrated individual, the agent may also be able assess whether they are talking to a person who likes to be in overt control or is more analytical, or whether the customer is driven more by emotional feelings or even the desire to be entertaining, and tailor their responses accordingly, offering the customer the balance of detail and speed appropriate for the perceived personality type.

- **Recognizing my value as a customer**
  Exchanging pleasantries over the telephone is not a recognition of an individual's value as a customer. Hard-won loyalty comes from being perceived as someone who is an integral part of the company success story – even if the company is struggling to make ends meet. When a call is received, a customer can reasonably expect the agent to know that he or she has been with the company for x years, that he or she has spent y dollars, that the individual concerned has provided valuable feedback in the past, that they have referred friends to the product or service, that he or she stayed with the company when it closed their local branch, that there were times

when the customer had to cut back on costs, and times when the company deemed it appropriate to give him or her a break. All of this should be apparent to whoever views the customer profile. If a company has centralized operations, but has not invested in centralized customer relationship technology, then it has lost all semblance of personalized service.

Investing in self-service facilities that make sense to someone as a customer is another aspect of value-recognition. Many customers today don't want to deal with an IVR script before reaching a human, so they will go to the Internet to see what they can find to resolve the problem. Many companies have already geared their online presence to attract the 'right' customers to the right online solutions. By classifying what type of customer I am – whether tech savvy, jargon-averse, analytical or otherwise, I should be directed to online information and functional sources that will make the most sense to me. This approach could include acknowledgment of useful peer-to-peer resources, including 'tribal' forums that are regularly visited by in-house subject matter experts and often do a more capable job of resolving customer issues than the company websites themselves.

- **Proactively following up on any outstanding issues on my behalf**

  During the course of most contacts, the customer expresses either a need to resolve a particular issue or may provide some indication of need. While resolution on first contact (ROFC) is often used as an indicator of service level, very often this is only applied to the primary cause of the contact. Adjunct issues and 'clues' may also be expressed by the customer. These are very often ignored or at best memorialized in notes made by the agent. However, from an extreme service point of view, these should be viewed as opportunities. By understanding the customer's predicament and issuing follow-up alerts, the company has a realistic opportunity to 'go the extra mile' and significantly improve customer loyalty. For example, an influential and high-value customer who rarely contacts the company but suddenly complains bitterly about a legitimate charge and demands some form of remuneration or compensation, may provide clues as to why he or she finds this expense so egregious as to warrant going to the trouble of finding the customer service number and waiting for an agent. By training agents to understand and interpret such clues, the opportunity to acquire a customer for life through proactive follow up may present itself.

Several companies have taken the step of following up with any customers who have expressed dissatisfaction with a product or service, not just to resolve the issue at hand, but to investigate other service transactions that are perceived as shortfalls. This can be replicated online through chat 'prompts' with customers who have been idle on a particular page for a prolonged period, or who have requested a contact from the company.

- **Taking my suggestions seriously**

  Associated with proactive follow up, this is another area where there is a real opportunity to build customer loyalty. For example, if a customer expresses frustration with the company's interactive voice response (IVR) and routing system, then send him or her a follow up communication that indicates their complaint has been noted and will be considered in future design enhancements. Very often, customer suggestions are provided in real time, stressful situations and are perceived by agents as personal attacks. The average customer does not care whether or not the agent is responsible for a particular situation, but merely wishes to vent their anger at a company representative. Those who actually can do something about the problem are often blissfully unaware of the bile that is being fired at the front lines, because the customer is merely seen as an 'irate' who needs to be placated, rather than an opportunity to gather important business intelligence and instigate retention policies.

- **Never making an unsolicited communication of any sort**

  There is a fine line between being perceived as helping the customer to obtain a better product or service and being an outright nuisance. In general, sharing customer data with third parties or using customer information in an attempt to solicit new business is the antithesis of extreme service. Terms and conditions which are sent to the customer via mail in six point type may legitimize the marketing process, but have nothing to do with customer service. Such tactics, which are also prevalent on the Internet, are rarely productive from a customer retention and loyalty perspective. It is time that many companies realize that 'customer relationship management' doesn't mean that they can manage the customer. In an era where social media can wreak havoc with a company's reputation, it is time to understand that the customer is now the one calling the shots.

- **Bartering my abilities for reciprocal goods and services**

  This requirement steps beyond the realm of 'normal' customer service. The concept of bartering in a contemporary, centralized customer service environment is truly ground-breaking. This is a major paradigm shift that is dealt with in greater detail later in this book. Suffice to say for now that such a method entails greater customer disclosure than ever before. 'Customer intimacy' – a term coined by Michael Tracey and Fred Wiersema and their book 'The Discipline of Market Leaders', was one of the three approaches to business advocated, along with operational excellence and innovation. By providing the customer with an opportunity to barter their skills in exchange for extreme levels of customer service, the company opens the door to a new level of customer intimacy – one in which the customer is willing to disclose more about themselves than ever before in order to cut costs and improve benefits. In order to achieve this level of service, it is crucial that the company establishes a bond of trust that goes well beyond accepted business practices.

This is real loyalty, and will be limited to only the most customer-focused companies.

- **Finding others with similar interests and experiences**
  This is another area that has typically been neglected in contemporary business transactions with customers. Instead, as discussed in the 'Tribal Service' chapter of this book, customers have taken it upon themselves to use the Internet in order to establish forums and discussion groups that can share mutually interesting and helpful information. Rather than treating every customer entirely as an individual entity, companies have an opportunity to become the brokers of this expanding form of communication, whereby users of the product or service in remote corners of the globe can come together and share ideas. By taking the lead in this area, a company can harness the collective power of customers with similar attributes, rather than being merely a casual observer of a powerful trend that is already having significant impact on customers' decision-making processes.

- **Advising me of issues that may impact my security**
  The establishment of trust is a crucial component of extreme service. While customers may be willing to give

up certain personal information for the sake of convenience, this comes with an implicit covenant that the company will never compromise that individual's security. To do so purposefully would instantly and permanently sever any bond that existed between the two entities. For example, in order to function usefully, contemporary customer relationship management (CRM) systems must contain certain information about the customer, such as demographic information, credit card and social security details, buying habits, financial outlay, and so on. Additional information may be purchased from companies who make a living by capturing in depth information about consumers. Any breach or suspected compromise of this information must be relayed immediately to the customer, along with contingency and crisis management plans that are designed to ensure that the customer recognizes the value that the company places on his or her security and is assured that the issue will be quickly rectified.

In summary, by placating needs for convenience, significance, self-worth and security, and providing a level of service that is unsurpassed, it is possible to attain a form of extreme service. What can one hypothesize from all of this? Firstly that the successful corporation of the future will engage in a mutually shared trust with its customers, providing them with all of the information necessary to make an informed buying decision, while gathering critical "Customer DNA" knowledge that will ensure conformance to the customers' needs. This corporation will be accountable for every action taken in order to provide a particular product or service, including environmental and/or human issues. The successful corporation of the future will recognize the insatiable characteristics of consumerism and will barter with the customer to ensure that a fair and equitable commercial transaction takes place, ostensibly at the local commerce level, where unrealistic demands may be more easily tempered.

Of course, it is naïve to ask any corporation to put its trust in the power of human reciprocity. Capitalist society is founded on a basic principle – you get what you pay for. The term "customer service" is most commonly applied to the act of providing post-sale support for a product or service. It implies the existence of a facility that acknowledges not all buyers will be entirely satisfied with a purchase. This sense of dissatisfaction could be something that temporarily interferes with the gratification process, such as inadequate instructions on how to assembly or operate a particular piece of equipment, or a service that was not enabled in a timely manner. Given that issues such as these can be rectified, companies may assess that minimal market damage has been inflicted. As such, the cost of employing a human (or programming a machine) to handle these problems, based on the frequency of their occurrence, may not unduly inhibit the overall return on investment.

More serious problems, such as billing discrepancies or faulty products, necessarily demand more elaborate environments. Some of the most powerful corporations in the world have massive customer service organizations, with thousands of dedicated staff and, as one executive put it, "budgets larger than the gross national product of Ethiopia". Yet because customer service may never be perceived to *tangibly* contribute to the bottom line, it is forever condemned to the "cost" side of corporate existence. No executive provides a customer service facility because it benefits shareholders, which ostensibly is the overall business goal. Given the capitalistic doctrine of profit maximization, such endeavors are not borne from altruism, but rather from competitive pressure and bothersome customer demands that can beleaguer retail outlets, branch offices and corporate switchboards.

Service embraces a far greater sphere than the "necessary evil" of post-sale support. To illustrate this difference it is useful to cite the example of a prominent corporation who used a television commercial to boast that their superior form of customer service is exemplified by a reservations agent who leaps over the counter in pursuit of a frantic individual who has forgotten a briefcase. The chase involves overcoming several obstacles, and ends happily with the return of the item to its rightful owner. Yet it must be recognized that such actions by the employee would typically be frowned upon by a supervisor who is measured by conformance or adherence, nor are they part of any training curriculum or job description. In fact, such impulses disrupt work force schedules and are likely to inconvenience and even alienate other customers who are just as anxious to board their planes.

In a human sense, the above examples illustrate a crucial difference between the perception of service and that of *customer* service. From an analytical perspective, perhaps the airline reservations agent, through some life experience or philosophical belief, had felt compelled to take personal responsibility for returning the briefcase to its owner, rather than alerting support staff. Or perhaps he was tired of the lines of irritated passengers and grasped the opportunity to bolt from his seat for a few moments.

Technically, the term "customer service" is most commonly applied to the act of providing post-sale support for a product or service. It implies the existence of a facility that acknowledges that not all buyers will be entirely satisfied with a purchase, for whatever reason. This sense of dissatisfaction could be something that temporarily interferes with the gratification process, such as inadequate instructions on how to assembly or operate a particular piece of equipment or a service that was not enabled in a timely manner. Given that issues such as these can be rectified, companies may assess that minimal market damage has been inflicted. As such, the cost of employing a human (or programming a machine) to handle these problems, based on the frequency of their occurrence, may not unduly inhibit the overall return on investment. That's bottom line customer service – the type of metrics-driven, uninspired interaction that we have come to expect from the vast majority of contemporary companies.

The realm of extreme service means embracing the entire end-to-end customer experience and even offering value-added services that cement a customer's trust and loyalty. This approach will become even more important as the balance of commercial power shifts from home-grown businesses to cheaper, faster, global competitors. The technologically-enabled contact center, with its appropriately empowered front line agents, ability to handle and respond to multi-channel communications, and adjunct customer intelligence, will continue to evolve as a focal point for customer interactions, employing ever more sophisticated ways of mining customer information and usurping the arcane 'cost center' mentality that is so pervasive today.

Tribal Service

The tribe of Ibn Khaldun regarded asabiyah, loosely translated as "group solidarity" or "community" as the primary principle underlying tribal society. For Ibn Khaldun, asabiyah arises from kinship, mutual assistance, and affection, and thereby forms the essence of tribal social life and culture. Tribal people live on the earth in a simple, natural way that satisfies basic needs, but they must maintain a strong sense of community in order to survive in the harsh environment...Most important (tribes) brought a direct, simple, and honest way of dealing with one another and the world around them...The longer tribal people associated with urban people, however, the weaker the former became. When tribal people came in contact with urban civilization, asabiyah immediately came under attack from the luxuries that weaken kinship and community ties of the tribe and by artificial wants for new types of cuisine, new fashions in clothing, larger homes, and other novelties of urban life…According to Ibn Khaldun, civilization needs the tribal values to survive; yet civilized urban life in most parts of the world destroys tribal people whenever contact is made.

Jack Weatherford

It is worth looking at the social consequences of the web-enabled world, as these are already affecting traditional concepts of customer service. While many companies may maintain outsourced call center 'sweatshops', with scripted responses and rigid procedures, and voice recognition will help consumers endure the otherwise abysmal queue times, the really profitable action will take place elsewhere. Knowledge is increasingly free and information is reciprocated today at a rate far greater than anything previously witnessed. The staid definition of "customer service" may remain for the frustrated masses, suppressed by increased shareholder demand for short-term profits, leaving others to set a new benchmark for excellence.

On the network, the traditional definition of customer service is already being tested. The real power is shifting to the consumer, as they hunt and gather online in a virtual tribal world. According to Rheingold, these 'mobile ad hoc social network' of tribes are enabled by "the combination of computation, communication, reputation, and location awareness." Not only will these influential consumers be valued, they may ultimately become anonymous, represented by software agents that mimic and learn their master's needs and interact as Anthropomorphs.

Customer service as we know it today will evolve into something far greater in scope. This will be facilitated by the growth of online communities where virtual trust is created by reputation and reciprocal behavior. Customers will increasingly consult these communal 'oracles' before attempting to contact a company in order to resolve a problem or make a product inquiry. Forums where both legitimized and self-proclaimed experts espouse their views in concert with both disappointed and curious consumers are already commonplace. Subject matter experts will seek to contribute to this medium in a restless search for recognition and identity beyond their physical communities. In the absence of contradiction, trust will be established. This trust will be greater than anything a company can establish through traditional 'best practice' customer service.

Progressive companies are already seeking to extend their customer service reach and reduce costs by contracting community and forum experts and influencers to become virtual agents around the world. When queues at the contact center threaten service levels, these 'virtuosos' will become part of the service framework, and their longevity will depend upon earned reputation from resolving customer issues.

Armed with the knowledge gleaned from online research, savvy customers who need specific outcomes will then contact the company and seek to find a human being who can resolve their need. Companies who continue to operate with twentieth century blinders by putting underpaid, undertrained and under-empowered representatives on the front lines will pay the price of dealing with the educated customer. Those consumers who have already subscribed to the notion that online communities and forums are far more trustworthy will return to those resources to report on their experiences in scathing terms.

These 'technosavages' are in search of self-realization beyond the staid existence of modern life, and as technology and competition from the other side of the world usurps the need for human labor, they will have more time to educate themselves, volunteer for community and local economy work, and barter with companies for products and services in return for specialized skills.

It can be surmised that the Internet has facilitated an opportunity to return to our tribal roots, hunting and gathering in communities that are virtually self-sustaining. Just as Jack in the *Lord of the Flies* casts away the bounds of his civilized self, painting his face, shedding his clothes and enjoying the kill of animals, so customers too can adopt alter egos on the web, transforming from civilized conformists into something that better fits tribal instincts.

Online social networks offer an unprecedented opportunity to systematically study the large-scale structure of human interactions. According to a 2013 study of millions of 'tweets' conducted by the University of London and Princeton University, there is profound evidence of tribal behavior online, including the development of language and communications that identify members of a particular tribal community. Apart from social group identification, the researchers found that there were significant opportunities for customizing online experience, targeted marketing, and crowd-sourced characterization.

In order for tribes to flourish in the virtual world, the basic service foundations of reciprocity, trust and cooperation must still exist. Those that are successful in this regard become the 'influencers' that companies need to monitor in order to minimize damage and leverage possibilities. This invokes the classic model of 'first actors', followed by 'early adopters' and ultimately 'bandwagon-jumpers', whose participation validates even marginal truths based on sheer numbers alone. The danger for companies, if negative influencers are not appropriately challenged, is that tribe members will 'swarm' around a concept or notion that could render permanent damage to a company's reputation. Mobile technology and the Internet will move such sentiments across the globe at the speed of light.

Taking this a step further, in the future we may see sophisticated pattern-matching algorithms applied to the textual and visual evidence of such swarming behavior in order to create associations with competitive products and services, in an effort to determine which one passes muster with tribal influencers. The power of such associations can be underestimated in terms of emerging customer-driven 'trials' of company wares. Perhaps it could be thought of as the tribal interpretation of Amazon's 'recommended reading' algorithm. The impersonality and relative anonymity of computer-generated critiques of a company's ability to provide meaningful customer service support could, in extreme manifestations, border on customer anarchy.

Even while the telephone is likely to remain the primary form of communication from a customer service perspective, and companies may boast that they are offering web collaboration, chat, visual IVR, speech analytics, email, messaging and other 'touch points' to customers, the fact is that the parallel universe of social media platforms, forums, bulletin boards, blogs and other media that exist beyond the realm of customer-to-company communications cannot be ignored. This 'shadow world' of tribal influencers is already exerting far more influence on customer satisfaction than massive investments in CRM systems. After all, giving the customer ten different ways to contact the company – albeit *potentially* convenient - is not likely to result in glowing reviews about product or service problems being resolved because of the fabulous IVR, or amazing web chat facility.

Ignoring social media rumors or the existence of scathing forums, while at the same time boasting about a state-of-the-art contact center and the number of customer calls resolved in less than three minutes, is not an unusual company practice today, as the 'call center as a cost center' mentality is still pervasive. As online tribes take root and exert ever more influence in the future, however, more companies will seek to install their own advocates within these communities, whose role will be to resolve issues, respond to unjust criticisms, and provide business intelligence on legitimate customer complaints.

Contemporary tribes are made up of people who are able to share opinions, ideas and behaviors even when they don't know each other. They will educate each other about a particular company's offerings by sharing real time stories, videos and pictures over every popular form of social media. If such information is corroborated by an adequate number of 'likes' and supporting testimonials, then the digital footprint becomes deeper, and the reputation of the company is moved or shaken accordingly.

Tomorrow's fortunes will be established by companies who are able to act positively and quickly on this behaviour, whether by rectifying a misstep or affirming an attribute for the benefit of the online masses. By accepting that these loosely connected tribes are driven by thought leaders who can have more impact than an entire multi-media marketing blitz, executives will begin to accept the fact that they are no longer in a position to 'manage' customer relationships, but rather must accede to the will of the masses or face a slow, painful elimination. In the words of the futurist Howard Rheingold "large numbers of small groups, using the new media to their individual benefit, will create emergent effects that will nourish some existing institutions and ways of life and dissolve others."

It is important to remember that we already live in an era when more mobile devices than desktop computers are connected to the Internet. Customers are capable of communicating anytime, anywhere to anyone who has access to the web. A bad experience in a brick and mortar store is no longer something that is an interaction between a sales rep and an isolated customer. A modern tribal leader who exerts great influence over popular opinion can just as easily be a dynamic, clean cut Harvard educated CEO of a major company or an anti-establishment anarchist who happens to strike a chord with a target market.

It is also worth exploring the roots of reciprocity, trust and cooperation, for these form the foundations of tribal survival, even in the virtual world. Reciprocity is an important part of game theory. As Robert Axelrod put it, 'the future can cast a shadow back upon the present and thereby affect the current strategic situation'. Axelrod found in a series of experiments that humans follow the same biological basis of cooperation as animals. According to Axelrod, "Cooperation, once established on the basis of reciprocity, can protect itself from invasion by less cooperative strategies." From this we can begin to ascertain the importance of acquiring customer loyalty by empowering agents to resolve customer issues with minimal fuss and bother. Yet today, the vast majority of corporations treat customer service as a cost and a liability, not as an opportunity to leverage proven human leaning towards cooperation, reputation and reciprocity.

Reciprocity and Extreme Service

Reciprocity is defined as a mutual or cooperative exchange of favors or privileges. Obviously, it is nothing new. Sociologists and psychologists have been writing about it for centuries. Here are a few examples:

Your corn is ripe today; mine will be so tomorrow. 'Tis profitable for us both, that I should labour with you today, and that you shou'd aid me to-morrow. I have no kindness for you, and know that you have as little for me. I will not, therefore, take any pains upon your account; and should I labour with you upon my own account, in expectation of a return, I know that I shou'd be disappointed, and that I shou'd in vain depend upon your gratitude. Here then I leave you to labour alone; you treat me in the same manner. The seasons change, and both of us lose our harvests for want of mutual confidence and security.

David Hume

Each individual act in a system of reciprocity is usually characterized by what one might call short-term altruism and long-term self-interest. I help you out now in the (possibly vague, uncertain, and uncalculating) expectation that you will help me out in the future. Reciprocity is made up of a series of acts each of which is short-run altruistic (benefiting others at a cost to the altruist), but which together typically make every participant better off.

Michael Taylor

When each of us can relax her guard a little, what economists term "transaction costs" – the costs of the everyday business of life, as well as the costs of commercial transactions – are reduced. This is no doubt why, as economists have recently discovered, trusting communities, other things being equal, have a measurable economic advantage. The almost imperceptible background stress of daily "transaction costs" – from worrying about whether you got the right change from the clerk to double-checking that you locked the car door – may also help explain why students of public health find that life expectancy itself is enhanced in more trustful communities. A society that relies on generalized reciprocity is more efficient than a distrustful society, for the same reason that money is more efficient than barter. Honesty and trust lubricate the inevitable frictions of social life… Generalized reciprocity is a community asset, but generalized gullibility is not. Trustworthiness, not simply trust, is the key ingredient.

Robert Putnam

In order to understand what extreme customer service should be, we must first look at the origins of the service concept, for long before massively centralized commercial definitions of "service", humans practiced a fundamental system of barter that we came to call 'reciprocity'.

As a simple example, for the past year I have passed a simple wooden structure that sits at the end of a long driveway. The structure contains two openings, one large and one small. These openings are usually packed with chopped wood. There is a metal slot above the openings, and a notice that reads "$20 Large / $10 small". The overall structure is aptly named "Tom's Honor Box". Sometimes, I notice that one section or other of Tom's Honor Box is empty. More often than not, some sort of denomination has been left in recompense.

Tom's Honor Box is replenished throughout the year – a testament to social trust. I can't help wondering what would happen if today's corporation were to exhibit the same level of trust in its customers? Revealingly, one of the closest analogies to a similar form of trust in the mainstream business world is the plain old newspaper vending machine. You put in the exact amount of money for one newspaper and the door unlocks. The vendor trusts that you will only take one newspaper. Of course, there is a great difference between firewood and newspapers – perhaps 99% of people only want one newspaper. There is no point in taking two or three unless you want to sell them yourself (which is hardly worth the risk) or give them to friends (which is hardly going to increase your influence). With Tom's product, however, the more you take, the more you benefit. Yet if a customer didn't have to put any money into the newspaper vending machine in order to get the door open – would we still leave the money? In the vast majority of cases, I believe that the answer is yes. There are always exceptions to the rule, but in a relatively affluent society the power of reciprocity is pervasive.

In truth, the shift from the shallowness of contemporary customer service to what we might refer to as extreme service, is remarkably straightforward. It is simply a case of getting back to the fundamental principles that make up a society.

No matter which language you speak, the concept of reciprocity has been a foundation of society throughout the ages. As Robert Cialdini wrote in *The Psychology of Persuasion:* "The rule says that we should try to repay, in kind, what another person has provided for us (i.e., we are obligated). There is no human society that does not subscribe to the rule." It is an exceedingly positive force in human interaction. In other words, if you are willing to provide me with something, unless I am a thief, I am bound by the laws of human society - actually *obligated* to give you something in return.

Typically this is a straightforward financial or even a barter transaction. In exchange for money, we expect a certain level of goods or services. The product must at least meet our expectations. If it doesn't work, or if we can't figure out how it should work, we expect the seller to provide assistance as necessary to merit the relative value of the money we provided. This level of expectation varies by customer, which is where *reciprocal norms* come into play.

Customer service is a company's best opportunity to create a bond of obligation with a customer. By marginally exceeding that customer's sense of fair exchange, we have an opportunity to create loyalty. A key to any reciprocal arrangement, of course, is the existence of *trust*. Without trust, business transactions become stuck in small details and complaints – the enemy of any customer interaction. It is from trust that we find the key to customer loyalty.

Sociologist Robert Putnam documents the decline of what he calls "thin" trust. Thin trust is the social or generalized trust that can be viewed as a "standing decision" to give most people – even those whom one does not know from direct experience – the benefit of the doubt. According to Putnam, when each of us can relax our guard a little, what economists' term "transaction costs" (the costs of the everyday business of life as well as the costs of commercial transactions) are reduced. Honesty and trust lubricate the inevitable frictions of social life.

It is not difficult to conclude that there are actually only a handful of large corporations who don't confuse the concept of Tom's Honor Box and the like with terms like "cost containment". From the perspective of customer retention, practices in the vast majority of contemporary customer service offerings are analogous to the Emperor's new clothes – everybody knows that they make no sense, but few are willing to admit that change is essential. In truth, contemporary "toll free" customer service is an oxymoron.

The Rise of the Barter Economy

Barter is also nothing new. It has been around longer than money. However, in the context of extreme service, mega-databases and the Internet are likely to forge a new form of economy. People will share not only items of personal value, but their human capital in exchange for food, clothing and shelter. This will be facilitated by enormous amounts of relevant data moving as fast as stock market transactions. A vast semantic network of supply and demand will emerge, and it will span the entire globe.

This has the potential to reach a point where every 'connected' human is given the opportunity to develop an online profile that lists every attribute that can be used to market their worth to others. This will consist of hundreds, perhaps thousands, of personal properties that make up a value proposition. These will be augmented by feedback from 'employers' and other references. As this massive database grows and becomes increasingly accepted as a norm, ancillary applications will emerge to tie the entire process of barter and exchange together.

Perhaps John Smith will start with his arcane twentieth century resume and start translating that into individual parts that make up an entire proposition. This will include biometric validation of IQ, academic and personality tests, certified recommendations, and every single property that makes John Smith a candidate for a particular assignment. A barter valuation for successful completion of the work will be assessed. This could mean that John Smith completes a project for a utility that in return provides virtual coinage which can be used in exchange for other goods and services. To maintain its value, only a certain amount of such coinage will be produced.

Sound farfetched? Not really, especially as computing power accelerates. In certain parts of the western world, the growing economic crisis has already helped transform the sharing economy from a niche trend to a full-scale phenomenon. While sharing cars, bikes and even clothing is already becoming as viable as buying, the evolution into human capital sharing and bartering is simply a matter of time. The thing about it is that it can achieve a broader impact with the Internet as both a stage and a platform. The web professionalizes barter of all kinds and allows it to develop into an independent branch of the economy.

Today, the concept is more grounded in collaborative sharing of goods. Here's an obvious example - why should cars stand around, unused, for an average of 23 hours a day, when someone else could be using them in exchange for other goods and services? The future question will be, why should motivated, intelligent individuals be unemployed, unknown and isolated when business enterprises on the other side of the globe can 'borrow' their innate and learned skills temporarily to fulfil their needs? No frills, no overheads, no complicated relationships and commitments – simply get the necessary work done in the most timely manner by the most qualified people, no matter where they are located.

Sociologist Harald Heinrichs has stated: "Shared consumption, in the sense of common organizing and consumption via the Internet, is (already) practiced by 12 per cent of the population." Social media encourages tribal behavior, and this will spread to a wider audience as western economies become ever more reliant on manufacturing from other parts of the world.

Metcalf's Law states that the useful power of a network multiplies rapidly as the number of nodes in the network increases. We already know that the number of nodes in the network is increasing exponentially. We can also surmise that the useful power of information shared over that network multiples accordingly. We've all seen outings where both young and old are too busy working and playing on their handheld devices to be bothered with boring conversation. Why should an influencer engage a couple of family members or friends at a local restaurant when he or she can address an entire tribe of followers?

The need for a company to establish trust among tribe members is paramount. This could involve providing your credit card information and other personal details to be stored by a chain of coffee shops so that they know who you are and what you typically want to order when you walk in and your cellular device triggers an RFID code that brings up your profile and preferences, as well as the amount you would like to tip for good service. In other words, the new paradigm of service allows companies and customers to interact in ways that were not previously possible, yet the vast majority of businesses are still providing pseudo service and acting as though nothing has changed.

As customers move away from brick and mortar for non-routine purchases, so too do they come to rely on those who are not part of the corporate machinery to review the relative value of a product or service. Viewing online images of a product is all well and good, but the real litmus test is the critique of others. The more members of the virtual tribe who take the trouble to provide feedback, the more comfortable the online customer is with his or her decision to buy. Any betrayal of trust, such as the posting of reviews that were obviously 'planted' by the company, is enough to send the customer scurrying away without parting with his or her capital.

For all that, there are really two types of tribes at work on the Internet. The first are the activists who have a lot to say, but not a lot of purchasing power. This group uses rudimentary, or at least basic, tools to convey their points.

They do not use the web to facilitate financial transactions, such as buying consumer goods and services. Instead, the web is used to measure the pulse of the 'have not's', and to figure out ways to beat the system. From a corporate perspective, they may be seen as trend instigators, but not targets.

The second tribe are those that use the web to expedite transactions – for matters of convenience, speed and cost. These are techno-savvy, relatively wealthy and time-conscious individuals. This is a key target group for companies interested in extreme customer service. Relying on aggregated peer feedback, this group places the value of corporate reputation higher than any other. In so doing, member of this tribe are willing to disclose more about themselves than any CRM system could possibly have envisioned. It is the essence of cooperation that makes a tribe function effectively, and in order to cooperate, trust must exist. For trust to exist, individuals must be credible. The only way to establish credibility is to openly reveal opinions, beliefs and character. Whether this can be translated to extreme service in the corporate sense remains to be seen.

Integration

Community, communion and communication are intimately as well as etymologically related. Communication is a fundamental prerequisite for social and emotional connections. Telecommunications in general and the Internet in particular substantially enhance our ability to communicate; thus it seems reasonable to assume that their net effect will be to enhance community, perhaps even dramatically. Social capital is about networks, and the Net is the network to end all networks

Robert Putnam

Much of the technology 'buzz' in customer service circles today concerns the rise of automation. The evolution of natural language processing and speech recognition, context-sensitive learning, web chat, virtual agents and so on provides fodder to those who believe that the days of the contact center are numbered.

It doesn't take a rocket scientist to figure out that the current labor-intensive form of customer service needs to evolve. For example, the best efforts of companies to defray costs by forcing customers to use Interactive Voice Response (IVR) systems are probably costing more in terms of customer anger and frustration than any other technological solution that promises substantial return on investment. As a result, the web is now full of helpful hints as to how to avoid the IVR and reach a human by the fastest route possible when dialing a toll free number.

A paper on the future of customer service published by a major technology company several years ago touted the excitement around 'seamless' customer service, whereby a caller on a toll free line would first be authenticated by voice print analysis – no need for account numbers or passwords – then be led flawlessly through a speech recognition interaction with an IVR. The customer would never be asked to repeat anything, and the IVR would be integrated with an 'advanced' knowledge base that would provide precisely the right answers at the right time. A 'voice tone analysis' feature would determine whether or not the customer was getting frustrated, and if so would immediately put them into a queue where the maximum hold time would be two minutes.

Apparently, this rocket-propelled queue would be facilitated by an advanced workforce management system which would recalculate agent requirements every fifteen minutes, employ sophisticated skills-based routing algorithms and automatically call in reinforcements from 'pay-as-you-go' agents who operate in a virtual contact center environment across the globe. Not only that, but 'accent neutralization' would be used to modify agent voices so that the customer would not be angry about being serviced by a foreigner.

As if that wasn't enough, the agents would have immediate access to an even more advanced knowledge base that would provide them with the context of the customer's interaction with the IVR or web and suggest even better solutions that apparently would need a human agent to interpret. Having quickly resolved the customer's problem, the agent would then be prompted to offer specific products or services tailored around the original problem or inquiry that would make the caller's life even better than ever. After the call, an automated customer satisfaction and quality assurance output would be generated based on the customer's voice tone and perceived stress level. A follow-up alert would be issued to the agent a few days later, reminding that individual to contact the customer and find out how everything was going since the last call.

Almost a decade later, some of this vision is plausible, some of it borders on the absurd, and a lot of it assumes that the customer of the future has no problem recording a voice print and interacting with a machine that is intended to behave like a human – a pipe dream at best. On a broader level, however, the most salient takeaway is arguably the notion of seamless customer service. It could be argued that for a business, the ultimate context for customer service is a world in which every customer touch point, from a visit to a brick and mortar store to an interaction on the web, to an interactive voice response session, to a discussion with an agent, is recorded by a CRM database and analyzed by a business intelligence system. The great challenge, therefore, is to know the customer and his or her needs intimately as these relate to a product or service. In truth, skeptics would argue that even if this were somehow achieved – and so much of it relies on human input to systems that can somehow parse freeform text notations – over an extended period of time it would probably bring in so many variables and irrelevancies that the customer would be become either paranoid or deeply frustrated.

Integration

The advent of social media has been accompanied by a lot of hype around how it will totally change customer service. From a channel perspective, that is somewhat true – the notion of customers instantly communicating their opinions via mobile devices to a global audience via Twitter, YouTube and Facebook is certainly something for companies to think about in terms of operational response. The question is whether it is cost effective for companies to ramp up their customer service support to the level where agents are tracking social media and responding to anything that may be seen as influencing a company's reputation. This is a prohibitively expensive approach and one which is hardly sustainable from a time and budgeting perspective. Rather, companies must be vigilant when an original complaint from one or more individuals is taken up by what Howard Rheingold has called a 'social mob'. The proliferation and adoption speed of social media 'flashpoints' spread via mobile devices is unlike anything ever experienced by the corporate world. Damaging testimonials can be seen by tens of thousands of virtual tribe 'members' before a company has time to convey an adequate response to the front lines.

The Future of Customer Service

There is also a very plausible business reason for identifying influential, high-value, repeat customers and making sure that these individuals are well looked after. Apart from their value as a contributor to the revenue stream, such customers are potentially significant influencers by virtue of their investment and loyalty to the company. Rather then, that the company segment these individuals and use every means possible to ensure that their tweets and posts reflect a positive outlook. Marketing, sales and customer service should ensure that CRM records for such influencers epitomize the notion of seamless interaction. Given the growing importance of a customer's 'digital footprint', this could mean tracking their handles on Twitter, scanning their Facebook posts, mining their LinkedIn profiles, viewing their sales interactions at the local company store, parsing their emails, faxes, chats and IVR records, analyzing their transactions on the web site, and particularly viewing their mobile interactions with customer service agents in order to get a holistic view of these key customers and ensuring that they are afforded premium service. While there is no direct correlation, it is becoming more common for top revenue producing customers to be more informed and tech savvy than ever before.

Integration

There is a notion espoused by some that not only will contact centers become irrelevant due to technological advances, but even that the telephone itself will become obsolete as a means of communicating customer service issues. All of this seems highly unlikely as long as humans need to speak to other humans to resolve their issues. Instead, it does seem plausible that the contact center will continue to evolve into a focal point for the entire business, rather than be mired in its traditional role as a satellite function. Given that growing numbers of customers will seek answers via the self-service web and online communities of interest before bothering to deal with the ubiquitous IVR 'gatekeeper', then front line agents can expect to deal with a more informed and determined caller. As such, the front lines will need to be better qualified and better informed before taking such calls. Reading from a pre-ordained script will no longer do the job.

Companies can also expect their customer service agents to spend more time on the phone with customers. The more knowledgeable the caller, the more likely it is that he or she has taken the time to get into the queue for a very good reason – i.e., that the answer cannot be found through alternative media. Agents on the front lines of the contact center will then become business differentiators who can truly add value to the customer experience. As a result, contact center metrics and KPIs will change. These will move away from operationally focused measures such as talk time and after call work, and instead focus on qualitative areas such as resolution on first contact and CSAT scores.

A particular area that should – but may not - evolve is the much maligned Interactive Voice Response (IVR) unit. Customer tolerance for endless menu prompts has been borderline since the introduction of the first automated attendants a few decades ago. The proliferation of centralized call centers during the 1990s accompanied the development of ever more complex voice response functions, as companies looked for ways to gain workforce efficiencies in what were invariably viewed as cost centers. By using recorded scripts to instruct customers to identify the nature of their call, hard-pressed center managers sought to show efficiencies by siloing contacts into manageable 'buckets' based on the training and – more importantly – availability - of agents. The auto attendant evolved into the IVR as computer telephony integration (CTI) allowed companies to develop self-service functions for inbound callers, such as pressing a series of numbers to access bank balances, place orders, and conduct routine business transactions. Customers who refused to interact with the IVR were effectively punished by being placed into queues with longer hold times than those who complied.

Poorly designed IVRs make 'toll free' calls anything but. The toll on the customer is significant, but even more so on the agent who eventually picks up the contact and is exposed to the anger of a frustrated caller. Today, there are entire web sites dedicated to advising customers on how to avoid IVR hell and get to speak to a human in the shortest time possible.

The truth is that well designed interactive voice response systems can be a great asset to customers who regularly call a particular 800 number. These super users can be on and off the phone in a matter of less than a minute, having placed an order or paid a bill. Interestingly, these callers may prefer to interact with the keypad rather than using speech recognition. However, the problem is that most customers do not make a habit of calling a particular toll free number. To these individuals, every IVR is the same – a painful auditory experience that will lead to long hold times while the caller repeatedly presses the '0' button in a vain attempt to reach a human.

For many companies, making it difficult for a customer to reach a human is actually a strategic business decision. The more a caller can be pushed to use other channels, such as self-service and online forums, the less headcount cost incurred by the company. For those that seek to ease the burden on the customer, but at the same time operate within budgets that make it financially implausible to answer every call on the third ring using a human being, the replacement of traditional IVR with visual interfaces that can be displayed via smart phone and mobile devices is likely to increase over the coming years. 'Visual IVR' allows users to rapidly navigate menus, view and investigate available functions (without having to remember a series of verbal prompts) and use a combination of speech recognition and point and click to expedite the call before joining a queue.

Another area of automation that is expected to evolve – and one which has lobbyists baying about the demise of human customer service – is that of Virtual Agents. This software is the forerunner of the anthropomorphic developments described in the next chapter. Using practical application of artificial intelligence concepts that were popular during the late 1980s and early 1990s, these online agents are given credibility through natural language processing and the ability to access underlying knowledge bases in order to provide users with relevant information. The next step in their evolution is the development of 'machine learning', whereby the Virtual Agents learns from the users input and retains that knowledge in order to target specific data that will be of interest.

In the near future, using more sophisticated mobile virtual agents as the initial interface with customer service will become more commonplace, as will the development of systems that facilitate seamless movement of relevant information between customer touch points. Traditional IVRs will follow landlines into gradual obsolescence as empowered customers demand ever faster and more intelligent resolution to their issues and requests. Companies who persist in operating contact centers as cost centers with scripted responses, unempowered front line agents and myopic efficiency metrics will be reviled as backward remnants from a bygone industrial age.

In the not too distant future, customer service is likely to take the concepts described in the last chapter a step further. In my days as a user interface designer with the AT&T Artificial Intelligence Unit in the early nineties, we were fascinated with the work of people like Marvin Minsky at MIT, as well as the Defense Advanced Research Projects Agency (DARPA), but largely confined to building 'expert systems' for large call centers.

Now we are rapidly moving towards an era when computer bots and intelligent agents start anticipating our needs based on our online activities. Major search engines have already taken this 'push' technology to new levels, as agents dwell on other servers and are called into immediate action by our desire for particular information. Using massive semantic networks, the search engine site then accommodates these marketing agents to present relevant news and product information in a manner that appears to suit the user's needs.

This type of pattern matching is not a new concept. It was a mainstay of artificial intelligence theory even before Marvin Minsky published 'The Society of Mind' and other cognitive science leaders advocated the notion that machines could emulate human behavior.

To some, this is an insidious invasion of privacy that smacks of a new world order in the manner of Orwell or Huxley. Rather than the user controlling what she or he wishes to see, the search engine itself has made that determination.

We already benefit from the fact that search engines index every document on the Internet. Using collaborative filtering tools, sites like Amazon go a step further by recommending purchases to us based on the choices of people who make similar buying decisions. What we can expect to see more of in the future are collaboration filters that go well beyond the realm of Amazon to encapsulate everything that we would like to see at any given time. This will be the epitome of extreme service, where anything that is of relevance to us will be gathered and presented for usage or rejection. The collaboration 'engine' will learn based on the choices we make.

At the risk of sounding like one of those absurd advertisements for romantic encounters, do you ever get the uneasy feeling that you are sailing through life while missing the lucky break that could positively impact everything? It's the sense that someone, somewhere out there, is looking for someone with exactly your background and characteristics, whether professionally or personally, but both you and the seeker are ignorant of each other's existence and so end up settling for less?

While it is obviously feasible today to 'pull' information about a particular topic from the Internet, and also subscribe to services that 'push' information out to you on the same subject area, this is an arcane way of staying informed. Each of us has a myriad of interests, but limited time to pursue each of them. Following your favorite personality on Twitter, scanning the online newspapers, subscribing to a couple of career sites, joining news feeds and looking up furniture sales does not help you to take advantage of a limited time air fare that was just posted, or find that job advertised this morning that is ideally suited to your background, or let you know that the piece of furniture you were going to buy this weekend is on sale elsewhere for half price.

Given unlimited time, web savvy and patience, we could probably find this type of information, but it is absurd to think that anyone could do this on a regular basis unless that individual was independently wealthy and indescribably bored. Using spiders, bots and other assorted web 'creatures' the ultimate goal is to find exactly what you are looking for in a time-critical manner, and present it to you on demand as a personalized dashboard.

This is not a new concept, but it is one which is being vigorously pursued by the likes of Google. Imagine the marketing potential of being able to find the right customer at the right time, rather than spending countless billions on mass media advertising campaigns that may realize a miniscule 'hit' on the target market.

The concept is simple enough – type or select exactly what it is you would like to know and send your spider on its way to gather information. If it returns with less than relevant information, then teach the spider to be a better scout by discarding some, expressing a modest interest in others, and zoning in on what really interests you. In truth, this type of activity takes enormous processing power and becomes dependent on the relative capability of the servers which are being spidered in order to function without causing massive congestion on the network. However, given the fact that computing power continues to increase exponentially, it is not unreasonable to surmise that this type of extreme customer service, driven by customers themselves, is eminently feasible.

Now put all of that computing power to work and channel the results into a wireless device that you don't even need to hold. Google is already using eyeglasses as a medium for transmission of relevant information. This approach will inevitably become 'old hat' as the biotechnological fusion of human and machine continue to advance.

There is, of course, a dark side to this new era of information. While this book concerns itself with the future of customer service, and thus views the intelligent gathering and usage of relevant data as a positive development in this regard, there are many reasons to be concerned about invasion of personal privacy by those who have access to the 'right' information. For example, portable software could include facial recognition software embedded in a microchip that could then be used together with a high resolution mini-camera to search for and retrieve specific records about a particular individual even while sitting in a coffee shop. In a positive sense, all of this brings to mind not so far-fetched scenes from the movie 'Minority Report' in which the customer strolling through the mall is shown personalized advertisements based on his or her known preferences.

According to the visionary computer scientist Jaron Lanier, "Counteragencies will gain information about agent innards in order to attract them, like flowers wooing bees. Regular netizens won't have this information, so they will attract no bees and become invisible."

Put another way, Lanier's vision in *Googlespeak* means that those who rely heavily on computers and end up spending money as a result of agent responses will become the focal points of new age marketing, while the proletariat continue existing in decaying oblivion, rather like 20th century libraries.

Steven Johnson in his book 'Interface Culture' describes several types of computer agents, including the 'personal', the 'traveling' and the 'social' types. According to Johnson, each implies a different understanding of human-computer interaction.

The personal agent is the one that is of most interest to those who wish to take advantage of the Internet without marketing interference, while the social agent is most useful to tribal protagonists. According to Johnson, "the real threat lies in the "traveling" agent, the one that unmoors from the host computer and strikes out for the terra incognito of cyberspace.

Anthropomorphic behavior, the "attribution of human motivation, characteristics, or behavior to inanimate objects", has been evident in some form on the web for years, often characterized by 'humans' who can be called upon to answer relatively mundane questions on web sites, using a combination of speech and written retrieval from sophisticated knowledge bases. However, the real power of this concept is being unleashed through the use of what could be called 'alter ego' persona.

This so-called alter ego may take the concepts already discussed and strive to add an important ingredient – that of privacy. This is the second phase of extreme customer service from a technological perspective, with the first being the power to actually retrieve the information we need when we need it most. This is also a concept that runs contrary to the notion of advanced customer relationship management, whereby every search, every web page visited and every second spent, and every item purchased by a customer is stored and disseminated to interested parties willing to part with their capital to gather such business intelligence.

Instead, the anthropomorphic alter ego behaves very much like an internet user who already takes the precaution of using proxy IP addresses in order to surf the web. This persona retrieves and takes ownership of information already gathered, shielding the real customer from detection and identification. Purchases will be made, not with credit cards, but with currency akin to Bitcoin, which also shields the owner from identification. This will be a major business battleground, as Google and Internet Service Providers act as the contemporary versions of 'Big Brother' while making it as cryptic as possible for a customer to utilize the web incognito.

So while the major search engines seek to make money by pushing 'highest bidder' information to the often frustrated user, the user-driven tribal society seeks to break this bureaucratic stranglehold by demanding anonymity, relevance, timeliness, clarity and completeness through the use of alter ego personal agents.

Peer-to-peer networking will be another method of retrieving information without disclosure of identity. Networked 'tribes' with similar interest will scour the web and share whatever they find that could be of relevance through folders that are accessed via the web, similar to the original concept of Napster. By linking large groups with shared goals in this way, potential customers will be quickly able to search the findings of others and use or reject these as they see fit.

Of course, all of this will ultimately come at a price, for while binary revolutionaries will continue to attempt to counter corporate web dominance, in the end only those with adequate funds will be afforded such freedoms. Lanier's counteragencies will be the 'haves', who can afford to pay the price for anonymity.

These will be the wealthy pioneers who are aware of the economic worth of their own information and will shift the balance of power from the supply to the demand side. They will push the envelope of extreme service, for these are the consumers who, according to Wacker, will "have so many choices and so much power that they will command the producer to provide the goods they want simply by withholding their purchases in a particular category until the solution they seek is available."

James Canton, author of *Technofutures*, predicted that among other things "computer-generated entities – will mimic human appearance, language, reasoning, and personality...agents will make online transactions efficient by virtually brokering, negotiating, finding, and communicating for us...the Internet will become a spawning ground for artificial life communities that will help us navigate in a networked world...artificial life will put an animated face, an "inter-face," on information, thereby helping us interact with devices such as the TV, telephone and computer...agents will adapt their personality to suit the individuals they serve...agents will complement humans in numerous industries such as finance, sales and health care...agents will replace humans in certain professional roles, such as entertainment, customer service, and education...agents will become a strategic asset for business, providing decision-making, managing, and planning services...agents will filter out communications, play with our children, search for information, and customize our shopping...agents will become trusted and intimate companions, helping us manage our lives, our health, and our careers".

Canton goes on to describe what he calls Digitally Engineered Personalities, or "agents programmed with complex emotions, reasoning and personality traits." According to him, we will choose a personality for the agent we use. This type of reasoning fits in well with the emerging tribal behavior evident on the Internet today.

Although still at a relatively rudimentary level, it is likely that the influx of Milliennials into the workforce may see the increased development of 'virtual worlds' for customer service. As an extension of virtual reality and online games, these online worlds populated by avatars will provide entire communities of service. By designing an end-to-end customer experience – pre-sales support, ordering, and post-sale customer care for particular products and services, companies will create programs that emulate real life possibilities by providing a unified shopping and support interaction powered by knowledge bases, customer relationship management tools, business intelligence capabilities, and options to communicate with live agents as necessary through video, chat, IM, SMS and voice.

Integration

By designing engaging user interfaces and a consistent look and feel, virtual worlds have the capability of becoming a significant source of customer service in the future. This means going beyond a clever front end application to permeating every customer touch point online. From example, the impact of having a space age shop front in a virtual world is quickly lost when the customer decides to venture beyond the immediate environment and retrieve product information or even use speech recognition to fill in a form that was clearly designed as part of another, more formal business application. Nevertheless, even now it can be argued that navigating around in a virtual world, talking to avatars, watching videos and following a virtual map is far more engaging than holding in queue for a contact center agent.

Without getting too technical, there are a couple of significant considerations that will enable consumers to use alter ego agents to scour the Internet and retrieve meaningful information in real time without compromising identity. First, the use of proxies - an Internet Protocol (IP) address reveals a point of entry to the Internet and can be used to trace communications back to an ISP, an employer's network, a school, a public terminal, and so on. Though an IP address may not identify a user personally, it is a unique identifier which represents a particular computer's digital ID while a user is online.

It is possible to disguise an IP address on the web by using an anonymous proxy server. A proxy acts as an intermediary, routing communications between a computer and the Internet. A proxy specializing in anonymous surfing, however, uses its own IP address in place of the users' in every outgoing request.

What else might we expect in terms of technology's impact on customer service? One emerging force is known as *augmented reality*. Unlike virtual reality, augmented reality takes real-world information and enables customer service agents to superimpose or overlay real-time relevant knowledge to help resolve a particular problem. Think of the *Terminator's* view of the world to get the idea.

Google's *Project Glass* is one of the more interesting innovations in this regard. For example, if the customer service agent has Google Glass, this individual could share a feed with the user, allowing the customer to mimic exactly what the agent advises. Conversely, the customer could show the agent exactly what issue is occurring. The agent could use augmented reality to physically show the customer exactly what he or she is talking about.

Canton describes these agents as "Intuitive Transaction Environments" - agents, voice, or video virtual personalities that get to know or discover what we want and seek to help us. The content or knowledge will "intuit" what we want, watch us (high-level gesture recognition, data mining, and behavior modeling), listen for what we are interested in, and help us find it at the right price.

Apart from Multimedia Webcasting, Canton also goes on to describe two other elements that he believes will define the future of e-business and customer service. One is "Deep Personalization", which he sees as "customized interaction based on a sophisticated real-time customer relationship management capability to build our online identity". Ultimately, the customer engages the online presence, and when interacting, the online business "learns" in real-time how best to meet that customer's needs. The online site then transforms itself, morphing into a content and interactive form that may be appealing to the customer. The online site then intelligently communicates and interacts, building virtual rapport and bonding with the customer. The other is "Network Communities", which will engage people with virtual experiences tied to their preferences and will be the next generation of changes that create competitive advantage.

As Steve Jobs once said, "...when (the customer is) connected all the time, it will put the consumer in charge in ways that weren't really possible before. They can get all the information they want, when they want, the way they want, on topics they care about. They'll be able to learn more about products and services before they make a purchase decision, and to research the price."

The linking of products with information retrieval systems through the use of facilitators like radio frequency identity (RFID), which store, send and receive information through radio signals, has the potential to further revolutionize customer service by providing detailed information about the item that the customer is considering purchasing. This is transmitted wirelessly to a handheld device and could include any amount of data, including source, methods, conditions, ratings, and so on.

Companies like Amazon already boast 'relationship generators' – applications that increasingly know you better. The ads that pop up after you conduct a search in Google are not by chance either. These pushy relationship management tools *infer* what you might be interested in, but in truth they are only acting on limited domain knowledge. Only the user can assert what he or she is really looking for, and this type of knowledge is gold dust to marketers. That's why it is so important that end users have a way of retrieving useful information from the web without having the interference of a thousand marketing bots clamoring for attention.

"As people become more and more aware of the economic worth of their own privately held information, they will come more and more to realize what a fortune about themselves they have absolutely pissed away.

"Therein lies the beginning of anger, and revenge," says John McKean in *Information Masters*.

The author goes on to state that "no statistical mode, no assumption from the average, no mountain of data about the mass market can predict how this one customer will act, because once you parse her at this individual level, you come to understand that she acts out of entirely individual motives. Nothing will lure this customer to move, because finally he moves from his own volition. That is why the balance of power in commercial transactions has shifted from the supply to the demand side, from manufacturer and retailer to consumer. This shift in the balance of power is also why corporations have to go where their customers are, one customer at a time."

It is not outrageous to surmise that the cutting edge form of customer relationship management may emanate from hundreds of microprocessors, smaller than the human eye can see, embedded in every item of clothing we wear, every object with which we interact, triggering wireless messages to agents which act on our behalf when it is time to replenish, or interacting with the web to retrieve automated updates on availability, new editions or styles, bargain prices on similar items and so on. The counterbalance to unsolicited commercial messages will be the use of 'friendly' agents which filter only those items in which we have a strong interest. Again, the battlefield will be commercial power vs. unwanted invasion of privacy.

The customer of the future will harness not only the power of robots that can comparison shop, retrieve items of particular interest, warn of digital intrusions, and so on, but also do it in complete anonymity. This is a paradigm shift from the days of the industrialized web, when centralized knowledge was the predominant domain of corporations. So much for 'customer relationship management', for it will be the customers who manage the relationship, not the corporation.

As Kevin Kelly says, "the cultural life in a network economy will not emanate from academia, or the cubicle of corporations, or even primetime media. Rather, it will reside in the small communities of interest known as fans, and 'zines and subcultures. In Future Shock, Alvin Toffler sets the stage: "Like a bullet smashing into a pane of glass, industrialism shatters societies, splitting them up into thousands of specialized agencies…each subdivided into smaller and still more specialized subunits."

Despite all this idealism and the notion that power has shifted from the corporation to the consumer as a result of the Internet, the truth is that power lies in that hands of those who control the display of information. A company like Google can decide on a country-by-country basis who gets to see what as a result of an Internet search. By logging IP addresses and remembering searches that emanated from those addresses, enormous amounts of personal information can be attained.

Yes we can afford to be more aggressive and arrogant on the web, but to a large extent we will always be at the mercy of the information masters.

Roundtable

The author led an roundtable consisting of several thought leaders and authors who gathered online to discuss the future of customer service. The following is a transcription of their discussion, without attribution:

TL 1   Customer service is not just a consequence of competitive pressure, although it obviouss helps. Fundamentally, all of us like to participate in processes that create value for other individuals. This is a large part of the human raison d'être. We like to see other people satisfied with the goods/services we produce, and customer service is integral to this.

TL 2   I believe that a distinction between the corporate definition of service and age old human-to-human reciprocity does exist.

TL 3   Of course it does. It's so obvious that I wonder why you are bothering with it. Nobody expects corporations to have human emotions, do they?

TL 4   The answer to this question lies in a branch of

evolutionary psychology called `deception theory'. Essentially, we are good when nobody is looking because internalizing goodness is less risky and expensive than cheating. This dynamic applies both to individuals and corporations.

TL 2   Along the same lines, one could argue that providing service for the sake of maintaining image is not "true" service. It is a fallacy. That is why call centers employ the minimal amount of people and implement expensive IVR/CTI systems to offload those annoying customers. Can we really equate absentee owner corporate definitions of service with conscious human desires to not only please others, but also do so in a way that is not damaging to others, such as consideration of those with minimal disposable income, environmental consequences, exploitation of work forces, etc.?

TL 4   We can. And in fact, we *must*. You think of this as bringing people down to the corporate standard -- I think of it as using a clear-eyed understanding of the wellsprings of ethics and the dynamics of markets to bring corporations up to the people level.

TL 2   In essence, you appear to be suggesting that "the invisible hand" of market behavior will continue to ensure that corporations will be forced to adhere to fundamental trading principles that will provide "service" at a level we can all tolerate.

TL 4   Given a sufficiently transparent market with sufficiently fast clearing times, yes. This is the real reason the Internet is interesting – it raises transparency and speeds up clearing times.

But my real challenge to you is more fundamental than this. I'm trying to get you to understand that the ethics game is not separate from the market game, and that to induce people to reliably play nice in either you have to understand that both games spring from the same predictable instincts.

TL 2   The underlying argument is that because corporations have no inherent interest in me beyond my ability to contribute to profitability, that they can never understand what it is that I truly consider as service, because it has ramifications far beyond the assumption of self-interest.

TL 4   News: *people* have no "inherent" interest in you, either. Or me. All of our "inherent" interests (including those that lead to trust and intimacy) are evolved tactics aimed at creating coalitions that profit (e.g. win the survival game).

TL 2   Perhaps I am mistaken, but it seems that this disconnection is having a serious impact on not only the "have nots", but also on our own lives in the short term.

TL 4   Whereas I think have an artificial disconnection between "self-interest" and service to others. I serve others; do you suppose I ever act except out of self-interest?

TL 2   So you believe that people, like corporate entities, are motivated purely by self-interest, therefore any market behaviors (such as "customer service" provisioning) and ethical behavior (such as social or charitable programs) are driven by the perceived demands of the most profitable customers. If these demands are not met or at least acknowledged, then the corporation risks serious damage, unless the product or service offering is in such high demand that service and ethical considerations are viewed as irrelevant.

This suggests that our hedonistic tendencies are completely dominant in today's marketplace. In other words, as long as it doesn't overtly affect me, then do whatever it takes to get the product or service I desire into my realm of existence. Let me take a seemingly extreme example - the fact that the money I acquire from company x as a consultant was derived from sales of a product made by a sweatshop on Saipan using raw materials made by a factory that poisoned a river in Indonesia, that in turn caused a village to eat contaminated fish, that resulted in the eventual loss of a rural industry and caused families to move into the cities where many turned to a degenerate means of making a living - is of no relevance to me because it is outside the sphere of my existence. The only salient point is that

I saw or heard about a product that, given my availability of disposable income, I really felt would be of immediate benefit to me as an individual.

Clearly, it is not in the interest of corporations to make us aware of the global supply chain ramifications. We are no longer self-sufficient communities, contributing to and depending upon local commerce for our wellbeing. In such an environment, hedonistic tendencies are tempered by our relationships with the rest of the community. The phenomenon of today's marketplace is an entirely new experience for mankind. My question is how then will we use "a clear-eyed understanding of the wellsprings of ethics and the dynamics of markets to bring corporations up to the people level"? Will it take a calamity close to home, or are we capable of figuring out what "service" really means in the modern world?

Are we not capable of rising above self-interest at all?

TL 3   Again, I don't think anyone should expect service to be provided for some kind of human reason like generosity or loving kindness. It's to keep customers and sell products. Courtesy ought to be part of the process because it works.

In regard to the damage to others, that is rooted in the nature of the corporation, whose charter is to return value to stockholders. I believe reform of corporate charters is one of the great challenges ahead -- if the plastic manufacturer was responsible for the 500 year life cycle cost of its product, it would have an incentive to design it better or to provide for recycling campaigns. But the plastic manufacturer is only responsible to obey the laws and return value to stockholders.

TL 2   My point is precisely that the reason that manufacturers are allowed to make, for example, indestructible plastic bags, and that corporate charters are so lenient, is because our concept of service is only as demanding as the society allows it to be. In other words, in an age of global capitalism, we are insulated from the effects of our spending habits. This suggests that our hedonistic tendencies (such as those expressed by Thomas Hobbes*) are completely dominant in today's marketplace. In other words, as long as it doesn't overtly affect me, then do whatever it takes to get the product or service I desire into my realm of existence.

Ford recently announced that SUVs were harmful to the environment. We already knew that, but it was not embedded in the social consciousness that is the driving force behind strategic corporate change. However, the fact that a corporation acknowledged that their largest source of revenue was harmful to the Earth was perceived as a novelty. Supposing every corporate entity announced the ramifications of their global supply chain. Would that change the corporate charter? Possibly, if we in our collective societal consciousness decided that such practices were unacceptable because they were extremely likely to impact our own quality of life sooner or later.

To me, therefore, the concept of "customer service" infers the total availability of information ("knowledge") that will enable me to understand the ramifications of my actions. If society demands this level of disclosure, then corporations must follow suit. Whether we do this out of pure self-interest or some altruistic ideal is not the point.

TL 6   Here are two issues which, to my way of thinking, seem pertinent. One is "permanence," the other "interdependence."

By "permanence" I mean "Will this company be around in 5 years?" There's no assurance, particularly in a world where business decisions are so often made dependent on quarterly earnings. There's thus a tendency to suck the customer dry: profits today are worth twice tomorrow's promises.

Moreover, so many people work in the "precarious" world of business that it may be that many have come to expect such treatment. McDonald's, as it were, has become the norm -- the slower rhythm of the waiter (a not a hurried, perfunctory server) has become something reserved for special occasions.

By "interdependence" I mean "understanding that what goes around comes around." Again, when there's little guarantee that you'll be around to get what's coming there's little reason to do more than the minimum. You, certainly, won't partake in any long-term benefit. This is a deep social problem, from my POV, for Americans -- the myth of the Old West honors individualism, not interdependence (the facts of the Old West, I think, argue differently, but one shouldn't underestimate the power of a good story).

TL 2   You are absolutely correct, of course, regarding the short-term profit making motivation of publicly held corporations. Such a strategy necessarily sidesteps the difficult issues of accountability and encourages functions such as customer service to be farmed out to lower cost service bureaus that basically pull people off the street to answer calls. There is no sense of loyalty in such a situation and turnover rates are so high that I have seen trainees pulled out of classrooms to alleviate excessive queue or "on hold" times for inbound customer callers.

Your words regarding individuality remind me of a quote I recently read: "It's nonsense to think that Americans are individualists. Deep down we are a nation of herd animals: mice-like conformists who will lay at our doorstep many of our rights if someone tells us that we won't have to worry about crime and our property values are secure. We have always put up with restrictions inside a corporation which we would never put up with in the public sphere. But what many do not realize is that life within some sort of corporation is what the future will increasingly be about." (According to Dennis Judd - Urban Affairs expert at the University of Missouri)

TL 5   I approach this topic from the perspective of a corporate historian who has seen the internal documents of a large corporation who not only was very interested in the importance and meaning of customer service, but also (to an extent claimed but which I have not determined in fact) pioneered the concept of "customer service at a distance".

And that raises point 1 in my mind, which is to say that providing profitable *least cost* methods for customer service is an important reason why the whole industry of customer-service-at-a-distance exists at all. If you can remember this far back, prior to 1984 the "toll free" or "800" number was a relative rarity and luxury. It was a major expense for many corporations who consequently only had a few lines installed to handle inquiries and for technical help.

When MCI moved into the 1-800 market the first thing they did was make it available more cheaply. The market for customer service then became highly elastic whereupon previously it had been fairly inelastic. That is to say, before deregulation it had been something like a $3 billion annual revenue stream to the AT&T Long Lines division; but a decade after deregulation, the entire 1-800 market had more than doubled to $7 billion. Not all of this was customer service, of course (e.g. 1-800-COLLECT). But a significant chunk of it was.

So the very first thing we need to understand is that the ability to provide customer-service-at-a-distance cheaply enabled corporations to provide more of it, and this in turn raised expectations among customers that more corporations would provide it. MCI, which was selling it, did nothing to discourage this expectation, natch.

In the larger historical framework, what we may be looking at is not the commodification of customer service so much as the expansion of the range of the relationship between consumer and producer at the expense of the frictional retail element (i.e., the infamous "middleman"). For thousands of years we have had consumers almost completely removed from the commodities that they were consuming with almost no real way of effecting any change at the point of production. The Roman citizen of Rome consuming cheap wheat had no real way of affecting the wheat-growing conditions in Egypt. His relationship was limited, at best, to the local Roman wheat merchant. But today, however, it is technically possible for more and more consumers to reach producers directly with suggestions for improvements on the products. I see this as real progress, and the future suggests even better results on the way. Corporations are genuinely concerned with maintaining "mind share" as market share now that they have a way of reaching people directly.

TL 2   I agree that many corporations are overtly trying to provide exceptional customer service using enabling technologies. I am involved in selection processes for over 100 existing "Customer Relationship Management" products for one company, and assessing customer service "best practices" via the Internet for another. What I find intriguing about all this is that while companies are determined to gather as much data about the customer as possible, the differences between the information received by the company (i.e., via the call center CSR), vs. the information actually recorded by the CSR, vs. the information applied from that data gathering, and vs. the information ultimately used by the company to better the customer experience - are astounding. Many companies operate call centers in highly inefficient ways. The actual analysis of customer interactions is hindered greatly by a combination of poor training, uncertain processes, inadequate intelligence gathering facilities, but most of all by an inability to understand the implications of the customer data being received. I see this as a major area of opportunity for improvement. Analysis tools like E.piphany are emerging as potential utilities, but clearly there is a long way to go in this regard. Regardless of the technology, however, I personally see the company-centric view of the contemporary customer as being generally arcane. The real power brokers are the customers themselves, and it is only with the development of an innate trust that savvy customers will open up to the possibility of a shared relationship. I believe that the Internet will facilitate this strategic change in customer-company interactions in ways that will turn the current model upside down.

TL 5   I agree entirely with your assessment of poor use of customer information and I wonder if part of the reason is that many companies use shared call center services in order to save on expenses. Ideally every corporation would have its own customer service center but in fact a lot of this is outsourced.

I don't know that the customers are power-brokers, but it is generally true that "the squeaky wheel gets the grease". It is axiomatic that customer service is in fact a routinely depressing experience. When customers are happy they are silent; you only tend to hear from them when something is wrong.

I'd like to see service reps empowered more though at the granular level. It'd be nice to call in with a question and have the rep say, "Gee sir, you've been such a pleasant phone call. I'm going to send you a $10 discount coupon right now just for being so nice." Innate trust? Unlikely. This is a paranoid civilization.

TL 2   Outsourcing certainly dilutes the customer experience. Once a company outsources, it is purely a question of operational cost - talk time, after call work, abandonment rates - these are the criteria used to pay the outsourced company - rarely is customer satisfaction used as a metric!

You are right - customers are not perceived as power brokers today. In a era of mass marketing, however, companies have certainly recognized the need to identify those who call, if only to build a "picket fence" around the top 20% (i.e., the profitable ones). Hence the proliferation of "customer-centric", as opposed to operationally focused systems. It is an exciting time in the technology arena, as e-business, customer relationship management and enterprise resource platforms are merging to provide end-to-end coverage of the corporate environment. However, I would argue that while these systems will become more and more sophisticated at capturing and analyzing key customer data, we are still in the Stone Age when it comes to understanding the capabilities, needs, interests, influencers and knowledge of any particular customer. This is information that constitutes what I would consider to be the customer "power source" that any company would give much to understand. In an era when 97% of marketing efforts miss their mark, coupled with an inability to analyze inbound customer touch points, companies are stumbling around in relative darkness, neither meeting their goals nor our need (as individuals with disposable income) to be "fulfilled" by a particular product or service. The "Golden Age" of service is a long way off.

You may be right about the trust element, but until customers and companies develop a shared trust, we will continue to operate at a very inane level of customer service, and companies will continue to waste countless amounts of money trying to convince the wrong people that they have a worthwhile product.

TL 5   Understand that I am more with you than against you in this item. The future of *good* customer service, the building of a new kind of bond between customer and corporation, is one of my major themes. Partly as a reaction to the dumb-headed things I saw around me in a corporation that *prided* itself on customer service! I might say parenthetically that it seems to me the burden of establishing a new kind of corporate/customer paradigm is as much on the consumer as it is on the producer. But, in general, what I was looking towards was a future in which the line between customer and corporation was blurred, where customers would be valued for their ideas and feedback to the point that they would become part of the corporation. Perhaps a useful analogy is the military where you have regulars and irregulars.

Perhaps the future of service is one in which we will have corporate "regulars" (employees and contractors) and "irregulars" (consumer/ consultants).

TL 6   Perhaps the future will find customers talking to each other rather more than they have so far. Consumer Reports began as one person's attempt to bring information to other consumers, but because paper-based publishing required centralization it implied an "organization" and all of the issues of time/budget/attention that go along with it. There are a couple places where people can get advice on what could be considered "consumer" issues (leastwise for home computers). As a corollary, one might expect that as people "become connected" to each other they will gain a mass (of collective purchasing power) that companies will find hard to ignore.

TL 5   As a matter of fact corporations would be well advised to *invent* this connection (via virtual community) and give it a home (via Website), because even a united consumer group is still a piece of market share!

It all goes back to how responsive a corporation wants to be versus how nimble and flexible it can be, to modify its products to suit the needs and desires of its existing (or desired) customer base.

For example let's say that Coca-Cola builds a marketing connection with its customers, who then unite as a consumption collective. But there is only so far that Coca-Cola can go in responding to their desires. If this collective were to say, "We don't want bottled soft drinks," then Coca-Cola would be in something of a bind, wouldn't it?

TL 2   TL 1 in his book makes a pertinent observation to our discussion:

The E-conomy has created a growing class of consumers addicted to the thrill of being able to get perfect products, perfect service, and perfect information almost as a matter of course. Customers increasingly expect perfect service and products delivered instantly...The E-conomy shifts the balance of power from the sellers to the buyers. Buyers are increasingly calling the shots, from telling sellers what their products are worth to dictating the way the sellers format their catalogs. Most of all, consumers expect to be presented with the highest levels of operational excellence. They insist on being treated as valued partners, as discerning members of a community in which they have a right to be well informed. The reciprocal of being more demanding is being less forgiving. Customers become less forgiving of sellers who, by virtue of execution or philosophy, do not embrace the new customer-driven model.

TL 6   But is it true? Or are customers becoming addicted to the image of getting perfect products, etc. -- if even that?

TL 2   The authors of the Cluetrain Manifesto sent shock waves through the staid corporate world with their pronouncements about service futures on the Internet, but we're a long way from changing the current model. TL 1 is really using the brilliant and innovative Amazon approach to e-business as his example, but I believe that we are still hard pressed to find other thought and implementation leaders.

TL 5   What TL 1 fails to grasp here -- or maybe he does, but not in that posted excerpt -- is that while technologies become *enabling* factors promoting social good, their existence is not sufficient to cause the good. Or, to use the old saw, "You can lead a horse to water but you can't make it drink."

What I see is a spectrum of customer-corporate relationship. The old mass production mass consumption paradigm will chug on. It never replaced the even older craft production local consumption model, by the way, just overshadowed it. So now what we will have is a partial return to the old model, only globalized. But not everyone will take advantage of their empowerment; some people will continue to buy products and services as they have always done. Why? Because it's easier, that's why.

TL 2   Technology vendors and their promotional resources, including most major business magazines, are doing a wonderful job convincing management that they have the "silver bullet" that is going to provide a competitive advantage, or at least keep up with the market leaders. Siebel was a classic example of an oversold product. Ads taken out during the Superbowl shows the financial clout of this vendor. Yet for all its potential, the original product was little more than a glorified contact management system.

The notion of driving change purely through technological implementation is clearly nonsensical, yet the time-consuming chore of driving process improvement and then using technology as an enabler is an idealism to which most managers simply pay lip service.

It seems to me that good old tribal reciprocity is a far more effective and less damaging service perspective than the contemporary efforts of corporations to become "intimate" with their customers. After all, the former approach was borne out of a genuine desire and/or innate drive to prolong the species. The corporate approach is purely hedonistic.

TL 6   Perhaps so, but I don't see how corporations are going to change their ways as long as their great need is to amass money. I give them money, they give me beads -- what else do they have to give me?

TL 2   As long as corporations can continue to convince the affluent middle-classes that the service they are providing is consistent with the goal of civilized living, notwithstanding the impact on the other 99% of the world's population, we will continue to endure narrow-minded proclamations of "world-class customer service".

Stephen Hawking describes "memes" (as in genes) that shape our thinking around what is an acceptable lifestyle. As those hovering around the top of the power hierarchy, we are not apt to change our minds about a Hobbesian existence. The rest, as Quinn says, can find solace in acceptance of their fate, transcendence, or revolution.

If all we want from a corporation is beans, thus relieving them of any accountability for actions that may be invisible to us in our insulated existence, then we will continue to subscribe to a model (a lethal "meme") that has caused more devastation to our "spaceship" in one hundred years than is possible for my addled mind to comprehend.

As an aside, I was wondering how you would define "customer service" in the ideal world?

TL 5   In the ideal world, customer service may be defined as a process by which the [physical, emotional, spiritual] environment is re-arranged to make the customer's world a better place in which to live either now or for the future.

TL 2　　One of the things I've been wrestling with is the fact that while we all have some degree of subjectivity on what we consider as "good service", there is a general consensus that today's brand of service usually fails to meet our expectations. The irony, however, is that those of us who work in the businesses that provide the products and services are the same people who express dissatisfaction with service standards. This suggests that the majority of us feel disassociated with the company's efforts to create service value. In other words, it is part of the machine, but not a part of our overall consciousness (whereas in cooperative environments, where the line between working and living is blurred, I believe that this is far less apt to happen, because everybody sees service as being an innate part of their existence - as was stated earlier: "a process by which the [physical, emotional, spiritual] environment is re-arranged to make the customer's world a better place in which to live either now or for the future".

TL 5　　I still think that the way out of the thicket of customer service foibles is to make the customer part of the corporation. I'll give you a trivial example. When I used to walk into a Starbucks coffee shop and saw some aspect of wastefulness, it never bothered me because it was *their* problem. Or maybe it bothered me, but only on some metaphysical plane. But after I purchased stock in the corporation, so that I became a part owner, suddenly the waste started to bother me. I'd point it out to the manager because it was *my* problem. More often than not they'd respond. Because being shareholders, it was *their* problem too.

So the first thing I'd like to see, is rebating customers with shares in the company rather than with specific products or services (or ... shudder ... cash). Because being an owner, for all of its dark and shadowy capitalistic overtones, is a great way to suddenly see things in a holistic light.

TL 2   Yet this "us and them" scenario exists strongly in the collective mind of both the company and the customer, despite the fact that we are the "us" during the working day and "them" when we are dealing with bills or trying to purchase something. When I was an employee at a major telecommunications company, I called the same 800 number as 90 million other consumers, and was subject to the same inconsistent service as everybody else, even though I knew exactly how the system worked. I had a vested interest in the success of the company from both a self-worth and security perspective, yet I felt so powerless to change its massive bureaucracy that I didn't see it as my ally, but as a machine that needed to be manipulated to achieve the desired result.

Perhaps that is the difference between Starbucks (who have a tangible physical presence in local environments) and the ubiquitous, yet invisible, corporations who distribute their products and services to mass markets. With Starbucks operating on a local level, with "real" and empowered human beings I can easily access (such as the manager), I feel empowered as a customer to make a difference, particularly if I am a shareholder. Here we are talking about developing relationships between the company and the customer, rather than the anonymous "encounters" we have via telecommunications media.

So would the concept of making the customer a part of the company work better at the local level? Could we talk about organized barter and reciprocity outside of the typical financial exchange? Could we use technology to facilitate this type of communal service in a larger sphere?

TL 6   On thinking this over, I submit that "good customer service" may not have "one" definition but be very situational. What's "good" at McDonald's might not be "good" at a better restaurant (leastwise you don't have to tell the customer what's on the menu!).

My wife and I (and kids) frequent a local Chinese

restaurant and have "our waiter," an older fellow named Mike. When we come in, the owner recognizes us and makes sure we get Mike -- we've been going there a long time and our definition of "good customer service" now includes Mike as our waiter. But I do wonder how many others have built this sort of expectation since the remainder of the waitstaff, by any objective standard, is probably as good.

TL 2   There are certain customer service situations in which we expect (and want) nothing more than convenience. While we don't expect the counter person at McDonald's to greet us by name or tell us that the crispy chicken is good today (although that might be a novel approach). However, there are other, relationship-based situations in which we expect a great deal more. This, I believe, lends itself more to our innate need for significance, self-worth and security. By acknowledging so-and-so's existence as an excellent waiter (customer loyalty), you expect him to reciprocate by taking responsibility for the quality of your experience at that establishment. Thus a strong relationship is established to the mutual benefit of the customer (Bob and his family), the provider (Mike) and the organization (The Restaurant). The problem with contemporary customer service occurs when we try to apply these relationship principles (a.k.a. the good old village store) to efficiency-based encounters (i.e., chain stores and cost-competitive corporations who experience rampant front-line employee turnover). Given that we live in an increasingly commodity-based economy, we can only expect this disparity to become even more pronounced.

I'm not saying that we shouldn't expect a certain level of decent customer service from efficiency-based businesses (i.e., basic courtesy and timeliness), but that we cannot expect people who are not rewarded or recognized for their efforts to show any real interest in us either. If these "sweat shop" employees provide good service, we generally attribute it to their organization (good training and process management), but if they piss us off, we will blame them directly (a no win situation for the employee).

TL 6   I wonder if there's a frustration level here that's sufficient to make one change vendors -- there has to be some empowerment **someplace** if the customer's valid issues are to be addressed. This puts large, particularly online, companies at some disadvantage. Perhaps there needs to be a "customer's service" organization in every community to handle this type of thing. Of course, Nordstrom's has its famous customer service guideline: do what you think is right.

TL 2   Despite loyalty programs and other efforts to retain customers, companies who create "pseudo-relationships" are always prone to losing customers to the competition. It seems that everyone is boasting about "customer relationship management" these days, but true practitioners, who actually use customer data to build a bond of mutual trust, are still few and far between, despite some serious software dollars being spent on technological solutions.

As you imply, Nordstrom can afford to empower their employees and develop strong relationships with customers because they cater to a higher income segment, allowing them to build in a significant customer service budget.

I've been thinking about the earlier response to the question on what constitutes "perfect" service - "In the ideal world, customer service may be defined as a process by which the [physical, emotional, spiritual] environment is re-arranged to make the customer's world a better place in which to live either now or for the future". I share the same viewpoint, although "a better place to live" is certainly subjective.

There is a tendency to view customer service as an event that occurs as a result of some problem or inquiry concerning a product or service purchased from a business entity. This results in most corporations viewing the service function as something that is not a part of the mainstream business process - i.e., it belongs in the call/contact center that we outsourced to x company for x cents per minute of talk time. Even those who clearly state that service is a key strategic initiative tend to put this function in a discrete box, rather than seeing it in the pervasive way that was described.

If we are to view service as something that enhances the quality of our lives now and in the future, then it is probably fair to say that "service" philosophy must pervade every transaction that affects us, even if it is not immediately evident. Akin to Edward Lorenz's theory that a butterfly flapping its wings in Brazil can set in motion escalating meteorological processes that lead to a tornado in Texas, so to must there be a consensus that, for example, corporate initiatives on the other side of the world may ultimately affect the quality of our lives as self-interested, if oblivious, consumers.

It goes back this sense of "us" and "them" in service transactions. We have adopted a more antagonistic, rather than cooperative, stance. The point about customers becoming part of the corporation is well taken. We are, after all, often remunerated as employees and consultants by the very companies that we take umbrage at from a customer service viewpoint.

TL 5   To be useful any definition of a socio-political concept such as "service" must contain some subjective elements. I was not being mindlessly vague in using the word "better". I was being deliberately vague.

The metaquestion becomes -- as always -- what is the good of the one versus the good of the many?

Arguably that really goes back to corporate focus on the difference between short-term and long-term profits. Why don't automobile service stations focus on automobile service and leave the milk, bread & video to convenience stores? Because the latter is more profitable, and retailers move to the highest profit margins whenever possible. But they cannot entirely abandon their core competence. So what you get is a transition from being a "petrol station" that sells milk & bread on the side to being a convenience store that sells petrol on the side.

One could make the argument that the service is a means towards long-term profit. But that would assume that the corporate focus is on long-term profit.

Which leads me to Point 2 about this item. The future of service will be crap as long as corporations focus on short-term profits.

TL 2   I am wondering about those non-subjective elements of "service" that pertain to the good of the one and the many alike, such as universal desires for security (e.g., advising me of issues that might impact the welfare of my family, such as the fact the local Novartis plant is prone to releasing large amounts of dioxin into the atmosphere), significance (e.g., advising me of items that, based on my buying habits and known interests, may be of value to me), self-worth (e.g., taking my suggestions seriously), and convenience (e.g., recognizing my financial limitations).

I believe that while considerations such as these are not on the radar screen for many corporations, the driving forces of competition and consumer awareness of impending limitation will produce a necessary outcome that is ultimately viewed as being for the good of all.

My question is that if this is true, what might the specific elements of universally acceptable service be, and are these unique to affluent society or the larger world?

Corporate idealism is wrecked by shareholders who have no interest in the long-term health of the company (and certainly not the customer). It is a fatal flaw that allows people to drive companies (and people) into the ground in the quest for ever-increasing short-term profits.

I recently read Robert Monks' "Emperor's Nightingale", which describes the ludicrous position that publicly traded companies find themselves in today. According to Monks, economics talks about "ceteris paribus" (all things being equal) – this is a naïve view in a dynamic world of Complex Adaptive Systems (multiplicity [ability to compete across several markets], spontaneity [forces that necessarily change a company, including innovation and self-organization], accommodation [putting personal needs behind the overall system goal (Cellular Automata)], adaptation [ability to change based on market demands], transcendence [rising above machine-like management], and ultimately metamorphosis [the edge of chaos – compare the drunkard vs. thrifty saver before the crash of 1929 – the drunkard ended up selling bottles to support the saver].

Corporations externalize costs in order to remain competitive in an era of commodities (i.e., instant information, free movement of currency, interchangeable domiciles for optimum production, universal availability of management talent). Externalizing is done via layoffs, inadequate pension reserves, higher medical costs, etc. to cause lower prices – short-term and often illegal strategies that cannot last. Such activities not only gain the attention of government (i.e., causing controls on both the industry as a whole, and often individual fines to corporations – a long-term effect), but also causes shareholder activism in the sense that the society is being harmed (today, customers and shareholders (more independent, more informed, more motivated, and more empowered) are increasingly one and the same).

More is needed, according to Monks. He states that "Putting owners in charge of what they own is the purest form of capitalism. Government involvement in protecting property rights is hardly socialistic...In addition to independence, trustees will need to have an understanding of the theoretical basis of governance. This will require an educational system that has only begun to be developed. The range of study will necessarily involve law, economics, management, accounting, ethics, and such other disciplines as may be helpful in understanding the role of commercial energy in a civil world."

Activist shareholders should ensure that management provide not only financial data, but also operational measures based on benchmark from best practice global concerns. Ultimately, the power will be to remove management if they are not performing well. "Too often the importance of shareholder involvement is dismissed because of their unwillingness and lack of qualification. The ultimate question is – can we afford a system in which the owners are not required to be responsible for the consequences of their ownership?" (NOTE: Yet who is going to set the benchmark among investors, who care more about returns than on ethical consequence? Do they only get involved when the government fines or censures the company for illegal dumping, human rights violations, etc.? – i.e., it has to be an entire mindset change – the need to perform human and environmental service as a matter of competitive differentiation. There is a presumption that owners want to live in a world that is civil, safe and clean – naïve?

We show little sign of wanting to break the stranglehold of short-term investment. Perhaps it will take a calamity or two.

TL 5   Beware of lumping all corporations in the same bag. There are big ones and small ones, family-run ones and transnational conglomerates, forward thinking and bottom-line focused ones. Like snowflakes no two of them are alike.

In general most U.S. corporations are run by management teams that exist in an uneasy divided mind between wanting to build long-term shareholder value and pursue short-term profits. Ironically it is the foment of the "new economy" (really, drive to market for the new technologies) that is causing the massive dislocation right now and forcing many corporations towards the short-term profit end of the scale. It is the logic of investors to pursue the highest possible return for the lowest possible risk. The problem is that while the former is quantifiable, the latter is often fudgable.

In other words: service is a cost. The payoff is quantifiable only in the sense of maintaining long-term profits. Management's ability to justify this maintenance is eroded because all corporations are in competition with all others for capital (except for those who aren't...) Investors cannot easily quantify the risk associated with short-term strategies. So investors invest in corporations that are maximizing short-term profits at the expense of long-term value. Therefore the future of service is crap. QED.

What will break the stranglehold? Courage. Courage to say "f-you" to Wall Street. Nothing else will work.

TL 2   It is unfair to portray all corporations in the same light. It's that "us" and "them" thing again!

"I think many people assume wrongly, that a company exists simply to make money," David Packard (HP) once said. "While this is an important result of a company's existence, we have to go deeper, and find the real reasons for our being. As we investigate this, we inevitably come to the conclusion that a group of people get together and exist as an institution that we call a company so that they are able to accomplish something collectively that they could not accomplish separately."

Despite such philanthropic views, however, the fact that many accept Adam Smith's "invisible hand" theory as the ultimate marketing truth (as opposed to his greater concern about corporate morality and ethics), suggests that we tend to discriminate between corporations only at a superficial level, such as "Safeway's service is better than A&P's", unless, of course, the corporation does something overtly terrible, such as having an drunken captain run an oil tanker aground in a pristine wilderness. In other words, we do not currently hold corporations to the highest ethical standards (perhaps because, as Kaplan asserts in "The Coming Anarchy" - "Material possessions not only focus people toward private and away from communal life but also encourage docility. The more possessions one has, the more compromises one will make to protect them.")

BTW. It seems to me that Robert Monks is corroborating your view that making the customer a part of the company (in his case shareholder activism) is the best way to erode the stranglehold of short-term investment based on unreasonable profit-making.

Also, David Korten (The Post Corporate World) states:

"Stakeholder ownership involves placing the rights and powers of ownership of productive assets in the hands of actual people who have more than solely a financial interest or stake in their long-term viability. Such stakeholders include workers, managers, suppliers, customers, and members of the community in which the firm's facilities are located. The very act of transferring the rights and powers of ownership from shareholders to stakeholders changes the very nature of the enterprise from an instrument of money to an instrument of life and community."

TL 6   Unfortunately, though, the history of communism suggests that putting "ownership" in everyone's hands leads to no one having enough of a share to care.

Consider: I went to a college where *everyone* worked in some capacity or another. Yours truly got a plum, showing films 12 hours/week, but others got tasks such as janitor or kitchen worker. We knew who these people were and their tasks were easier because, well, we didn't want it to be any worse than it had to be. The net result was to keep college costs down.

In most colleges, there's the implicit knowledge that keeping the workload down keeps the price down (and generally an explicit plea by housekeeping to that effect), but is this knowledge of a direct financial relationship influence student behavior very much? Doubtful.

This leads me to think that there's an important scaling/ownership issue involved.

TL 2   Here's a relevant excerpt from Christopher Locke in the Cluetrain Manifesto:

"The question is whether, as a company, you can afford to have more than an advertising jingle persona. Can you put yourself out there: say what you think in your own voice, present who you really are, show what you really care about? Do you have any genuine passion to share? Can you deal with such honesty? Such exposure? Human beings are often magnificent in this regard, while companies, frankly, tend to suck. For most corporations, even considering these questions - and they're being forced to do so by both Internet and intranet - is about as exciting as the offer of an experimental brain transplant...Companies that are harming themselves out of ignorance can, with a little humility and a lot of hard work, begin to learn and change. I've seen it happen, and it's an impressive thing. On the other hand, companies that are harming the people who work for them out of cowardice, greed, and willful stupidity richly deserve whatever fate may have in store."

Based on our discussion, is Locke being naive? His views would be embraced by complexity science, which suggests that (according to Roger Lewin) "In complex adaptive systems, agents interact, and when they have a mutual effect on one another something novel emerges. Anything that enhances these interactions will enhance the creativity and adaptability of the system. In human organizations this translates into agents as people, and interactions with mutual effect as being relationships that are grounded in a sense of mutuality: people share a mutual respect, and have a mutual influence and impact on each other. From this emerged genuine care. Care is not a thing but an action – to be care-full – to care about your work, to care for fellow workers, to care for the organization, to care about the community."

These sentiments, if embraced by corporations, present a hopeful future for service. However, it's difficult to envision our industrial age corporate model allowing any such approach. As was stated earlier, as long as short-term profit-making is allowed to dictate corporate strategy, then we can expect lousy service.

If we take an idealist position, it would mean that companies adopt a credo akin to that of Robert W. Johnson, Jr., son of the man who founded Johnson & Johnson, who described "enlightened self-interest" that put service to customers first, service to employees and to management second and third, service to communities fourth, and service to stockholders, last. "When these things have been done," he wrote. "The stockholders should receive a fair return."

TL 5   There is the air, or aura, of a social reformer about you. But take it from the sour voice of reason: any system, any mechanism that you may advocate that does not account for the natural inclination of most human beings towards a modicum of avarice, sloth and gluttony is doomed to failure.

TL 2   No doubt that we all have some disposition towards all of those "deadly" attributes.

However, is the current climate not a product of a contemporary economic assumption that in an affluent society, our "raison d'être" is purely the accumulation of wealth (as opposed to the more ethereal goals of Maslow's hierarchy)? Although avarice, sloth and gluttony were just as prone to exist in tribal society, it is unlikely that a community striving merely to produce food enough to exist would have tolerated such behaviors for long. Perhaps the excesses of civilization allow us to indulge in these tendencies, and more so than ever in post-industrial society, but if we are to believe in natural selection, then these cannot last indefinitely (as if we didn't know that!).

Jeremy Seabrook wrote a book entitled "What Went Wrong? Why Hasn't Having More Made People Happier?" (1978 - that seems like an awfully long time ago). In it, he describes the plight of children in modern society as follows:

"The child tends to be stripped of all social influences

but those of the market place, all sense of place, function and class is weakened, the characteristics of region and clan, neighborhood or kindred are attenuated. The individual is denuded of everything but appetites, desires and tastes, wrenched from any context of human obligation or commitment. It is a process of mutilation; and once this has been achieved, we are offered the consolation of reconstituting the abbreviated humanity out of the things and goods around us, and the fantasies and vapors which they emit. A culture becomes the main determinant upon morality, beliefs, and purposes, usurping more and more territory that formerly belonged to teachers, parents, community, priests and politics alike."

All right, so maybe this is a little too much. However, I believe that the future of corporate success will be based around using technology to share mutually beneficial information between both the company and the customer, to demonstrate corporate accountability for activities that may compromise the quality of human existence, and to fully grasp the fact that the employee and the customer are one in the same and deserve to be treated as such.

TL 6   To play a Hegelian, perhaps the issue here is partly one of existing in a system which lacks a proper counterweight. The organized activity of a corporation allows it to act in ways which are antagonistic to the needs/wants of its customers --

who are voiceless, perhaps, due to a lack of organizing, enabling, technology.

TL 2   The authors of the Cluetrain believe that they have the answer to this problem:

"In fact, the news gets better from here on out. And the first bit of news is that this isn't about us and them. It's about us. "Them" don't exist. Not really. Corporations are legal fictions, willing suspensions of disbelief. Pry the roof off any company and what do you find inside? The cracker jack prize is ourselves, just ordinary people...Inside, outside, there's a conversation going on today that wasn't happening at all five years ago and hasn't been very much in evidence since the industrial revolution began. Now, spanning the planet via the Internet, this conversation is so vast, so multifaceted, that trying to figure what it's about is futile...For the defenseless position you companies all find yourselves in, you can thank the creators of the Internet."

For all this unbridled enthusiasm, one can hardly imagine that the Internet in its current form will be viewed by traditionalists as anything but one more potential marketing, sales and service channel - something for the major institutions to manipulate and control.

Yet perhaps the emergence of sophisticated

software agents will change all that. Perhaps such virtual entities, acting on our behalf, will help us overcome the barrier preventing us from developing a mutual trust between individuals and the faceless corporation. Perhaps it is only then that we will realize the type of cooperation that will put today's antiquated service principles behind us.

TL 6   Another issue: how much service is a person willing to pay for (as a hidden cost) versus how much a person is willing to pay for as a revealed cost -- perhaps a service fee mark-up?

It seems to me that two extremes are particularly bad at customer service: companies that sell a product and don't really expect return purchasers and companies that have you locked in (like the electric company). In the middle, perhaps if we knew (and the company knew we knew) that "x" amount was allocated to customer service perhaps both company and consumer would have a better handle on how much to expect out of the relationship.

TL 2   Perhaps we can objectively recognize whether the goal of the business is to provide excellent service (thereby justifying a higher price) or simply to compete on price. As Heskett demonstrated in "The Service Profit Chain", it's often not so much the amount of money a company overtly budgets for customer service, but the value that the company places on its employees.

On the surface, I think that it is fair to say that a customer who buys clothes at a non-trendy warehouse outlet accepts the fact that nobody is going to help them, that the clothes will be strewn around all over the place, and that the only objective is to pick up a bargain. There's really not much point in complaining about the service.

On the other hand, the customer who goes into Nordstrom's is willing to pay a premium (even if they could get the same item for less elsewhere) for reasons of significance and self-worth. When you pay that sort of price, you really would be justified in complaining about customer service.

However, the employees at Nordstrom's are incented to really give the customer a good experience - as you said "do what you think is right".

If that distinction is blurred, or we start seeing everything as a commodity (as in the case of the AT&T/MCI/Sprint $100 coupon for switching debacle of a couple of decades ago) then we rapidly become disgruntled. AT&T's customer service budget, for example, was greater than the GNP of Ethiopia, yet no one is writing about how terrific they are at helping customers.

The problem becomes really pronounced when we as consumers make no distinction between our wonderful experience at Nordstrom's and the woefully slow and rude DMV counter person. The latter individual is not motivated to provide any kind of service at all. Heskett would describe this monopolistic situation as one in which we are "hostages" (i.e., no choice but grin and bear it), as opposed to Nordstrom's, where we become "Apostles" (i.e., highly loyal and highly satisfied).

Companies who do not innately view service as a strategic differentiator will match the competition and nothing more. They will never disclose how much service (or lack thereof) we can expect because such a precedent exposes them to all sorts of competitive criticism.

Conclusion

The ultimate purpose of business is not, or should not be, simply to make money. Nor is it merely a system of making and selling things. The promise of business is to increase the well-being of humankind through service, a creative invention and ethical philosophy.

Paul Hawken

Industrialized societies are becoming a little weary of the constant promise of the service "ideal". It seems we can't get enough of saying the same thing in different ways. Yet for all that, are we really on the cusp of seeing a customer service revolution?

We still wait in seemingly interminable telephone queues, hear the same platitudes about how important our call must be, often deal with aggressive sales people, argue with disinterested service providers, and fret about missed installation appointments. There are, of course, exceptions, but these often occur because for a short period of time, a marketing executive or CEO decided to make service realization his or her competitive platform.

Some would even argue that given the increasingly brittle nature of environmental, political, social and economic structures, that affluent and influential individuals must now insist not just upon personalized service, but for product and service providers to take absolute responsibility for the global consequences of their actions. It could be argued that any human who has transcended the basic physiological needs of food, clothing and shelter is in a position to question the methods by which companies bring their goods and services to market. Those companies who exercise the greatest humanistic and environment awareness without passing excessive costs on to the consumer could someday be regarded as the "true" service providers, while those who boast "customer service" only to those with purchasing power, will be relegated to the realm of Milton Friedman's proverbial hypocrites.

We could hypothesize that, for example, we are drawn from our routine oblivion by some local calamity, such as the poisoning of groundwater, a massive chemical explosion, a concentrated occurrence of leukemia, a deadly food-borne bacteria, prolonged and deadly air pollution, a crash of the telecommunications system, or the failure of the power grid. In all likelihood, such events would arouse different responses from those affected. Some may simply accept that sometimes things happen that are out of our control. Others would actively seek to rectify the situation and, if the situation was not a result of force majeure, punish the perpetrators.

Yet what if the realization was reached that we had let things go so far that they could never be rectified? Then we may all take a different and highly reactionary view. We would fervently wish that we could return to 'normality'. We would probably wish that as a society, we had been more aware of the consequences.

For all that, as David Packard espoused, treat people with respect, whether they are considered employees or customers, and the corporation will reap the benefits. Respect means providing the best product or service that you possibly can, and fixing any unforeseen problems as capably as you can, while still accruing financial gains relative to the amount of effort (both past and present) that you have assigned to the endeavor.

With globalization, more and more companies are competing for fewer and fewer niche markets, and workers from highly industrialized nations are being displaced by just as hard-working and intelligent, yet less expensive, workers from emerging economies. In other words, the balance of commercial power is shifting to providers many of whom cannot yet purchase many of the goods they make.

The basic premise of this book has been that, notwithstanding economic power shifts, the pervasive reach, increasing usage, expanding power and speed of online communications means that companies will have to work a lot harder in the future to monitor the 'customer experience', in order to control damage and seize opportunity. We are seeing a paradigm shift away from traditional concepts of 'customer service' and into a high speed world where connected customers will have global access to both advocates and antagonists. Such customers will not tolerate lengthy hold times, endless menus, scripted responses and unempowered company representatives without venting their frustration on 'tribal' forums and social media platforms.

Conclusion

Of course, despite the phenomenal power of the Internet to educate and empower customers, much will be contingent on the future control exerted by governments and search engine provisioners. As this book goes to print, for example, rumors are rife about a U.N. sponsored capability to control the Internet as considered necessary to censor 'malicious' information – a 'kill switch' so to speak. Other rumors swirl around the influence of big business on search engine results displayed by companies like Google. As the largest Internet search engine in the world today, Google's own information gathering and data mining activities are also under scrutiny. Suppression will become a key point of contention in the future, as will anonymity and individualized data gathering. Already, akin to an Orwellian vision, many global consumers surfing the net are prone to seeing only what the powers that be want those individuals to see.

Will these conflicting agendas result in a clear winner? On the one hand, tighter controls on Internet content will retard the demise of pseudo service, while on the other, companies will be forced to adopt at least some of the concepts of extreme service in order to enhance or at least maintain a positive reputation among the increasingly important online 'influencers'.

Obviously, many variables may come into play that will shape the future of customer service. Global events, power shifts, suppression and control, may render several of the concepts discussed in this book at least somewhat moot. Perhaps we are living in the golden age of service now, and just don't know it! The fact is that we are never going to be fully satisfied with any service model. However, it is apparent that companies who ignore the reach, impatience and potential 'clout' of the Internet-enabled customer of the future will do so at their ever increasing peril.

CPSIA information can be obtained at www.ICGtesting.com
Printed in the USA
LVOW10s1756080913

351507LV00022B/257/P

9 781482 065732